The
CHALLENGE
and the
HARVEST

FRANKLIN D. RICHARDS

The
CHALLENGE
and the
HARVEST

Deseret Book Company
Salt Lake City, Utah

With appreciation to my wife, Helen Kearnes Richards; my secretary, Glenna Reese; the president of Deseret Book, Lowell M. Durham, Jr.; and editors Eleanor Knowles and Jack Lyon.

First printing February 1983

Contents

Adversity

Gratitude for Difficulties

It's human nature to want to follow the easy paths, but each of us should thank the Lord for the difficulties we encounter. I know that as we reflect back upon our lives we will acknowledge that those experiences that were the most difficult were, in the end, the most profitable. The lessons learned and faith developed in such hours of hardship prove to be of eternal value to us in our path of eternal progress.

Many of us recall the dark days of the depression in the early thirties. The loss of one's possessions is a humbling experience, especially with the responsibilities of a family, but the lessons will never be forgotten.

Likewise, the loss of a loved one is a sad experience, but this difficult test builds faith, courage, and humility. In the presence of death we are made humble, for then we realize our own helplessness and our dependence upon our Heavenly Father for comfort.

Those who have fulfilled missions understand the difficulties and disappointments in bringing souls into the kingdom of God. But none would deny the great opportunities for personal growth and development as well as eternal joy and happiness.

Service to mankind through activity in the Church affords one of the finest opportunities for experience. This type of experience develops love, faith, wisdom, understanding, discernment, and, invariably, increased knowledge.

The Necessity for Adversity

When Adam was cast out of the Garden of Eden he was told, "In the sweat of thy face shalt thou eat bread, till thou return unto the ground; for out of it wast thou taken." (Gen. 3:19.)

I am told that over the entrance to a great European university campus there is an inscription that says that "nothing worthwhile ever comes to a person except by the anguish of his soul and the sweat of his brow."

Ella Wheeler Wilcox, in her beautiful poem titled "Gethsemane," expressed it this way:

> All those who journey, soon or late,
> Must pass within the garden's gate;
> Must kneel alone in darkness there,
> And battle with some fierce despair.
> God pity those who cannot say,
> "Not mine, but thine," who only pray,
> "Let this cup pass," and cannot see
> The purpose in Gethsemane.

Although it is not customary for one to seek out difficult or unpleasant experiences, it is true that the trials and tribulations of life that stand in the way of man's growth and development become stepping-stones by which he climbs to greater heights —provided, of course, that he does not permit them to discourage him.

The story of most men and women who attain a degree of greatness and achievement is generally the story of a person overcoming handicaps. It appears that there are lessons that can only be learned through the overcoming of obstacles.

Zion's Camp

Two of the most interesting and trying experiences of this dispensation are those of Zion's Camp and Liberty Jail, both of

which not only influenced the lives of great men, but also greatly affected the history of the Church.

When the members of the Church in Missouri were being
persecuted, the Prophet Joseph Smith made it a matter of
prayer. He received a revelation on February 24, 1834. The
Lord instructed him to assemble at least one hundred men and
to go to the land of Zion, or Missouri. (D&C 103:34.)

Zion's Camp, a group of approximately one hundred and
fifty men, gathered at Kirtland, Ohio, in the spring of 1834 and
marched to western Missouri. By the time they reached Missouri, the camp had increased to approximately two hundred
men. The purposes of the trek were to join the Saints in Missouri, buy lands in Jackson County and surrounding counties,
and retrieve land taken by the mobs that had dispossessed the
Missouri Saints of considerable of their property.

The men reached Missouri, where, after extensive negotia-
tions with Governor Dunklin failed to produce results, Zion's
Camp was disbanded; it was felt advisable to await some future
opportunity for the redemption of Zion. Most of those who had
formed Zion's Camp returned to Kirtland, which was, at that
time, the center of ecclesiastical activity.

The journey covered more than one thousand miles, with
dissensions within and hostile demonstrations from without.
There were hardships and disappointments, but these experiences had real value because from this group many became
leaders in the exodus of twelve thousand people from Missouri
to Nauvoo. Then later, many became leaders in the great
western exodus from Nauvoo to the Salt Lake Valley.

The journey of Zion's Camp was regarded by many as an un-
profitable and unsuccessful episode. A brother in Kirtland who
did not go with the camp, meeting Brigham Young upon his return, said to him, "Well, what did you gain on this useless journey to Missouri with Joseph Smith?" "All we went for,"
promptly replied Brigham Young. "I would not exchange the
experience I gained on the expedition for all the wealth in

Geauga County," the county in which Kirtland was located. (B. H. Roberts, "Brigham Young, a Character Sketch," *Improvement Era* 6:567.)

In February 1835, those brethren who had accompanied the Prophet Joseph to Missouri as members of Zion's Camp were called together, and from their numbers, the Quorums of the Twelve and the Seventies were chosen. The Prophet explained that the trials and tribulations endured by the members of Zion's Camp were not in vain, "and it was the will of God that those who went to Zion, with a determination to lay down their lives, if necessary, should be ordained to the ministry, and go forth to prune the vineyard for the last time." (*History of the Church* 2:182.)

In the light of these events, it is evident that the Zion's Camp experiences were of immense value to both the individuals involved and the Church.

Liberty Jail

The Lord gave to the Prophet Joseph Smith, while he was imprisoned in Liberty Jail, a great revelation. Liberty Jail for a time became a center of instruction.

Elder Brigham H. Roberts in the *Comprehensive History of the Church* (1:526) says: "The eyes of the saints were turned to it [Liberty Jail] as the place whence would come encouragement, counsel—the word of the Lord. It was more temple than prison, so long as the Prophet was there. It was a place of meditation and prayer. A temple, first of all, is a place of prayer; and prayer is communion with God. It is the 'infinite in man seeking the infinite in God.' Where they find each other, there is holy sanctuary—a temple. Joseph Smith sought God in this rude prison, and found him. Out of the midst of his tribulations he called upon God in passionate earnestness."

The answer came as God replied, "My son, peace be unto thy soul; thine adversity and thine afflictions shall be but a small moment; and then, if thou endure it well, God shall exalt thee on high." (D&C 121:7-8.)

The Prophet was told that if great tribulation should beset him, and even "if the very jaws of hell shall gape open the mouth wide after thee, know thou my son, that all these things shall give thee experience, and shall be for thy good. The Son of Man hath descended below them all. Art thou greater than he?" (D&C 122:7-8.)

A Lesson on Priesthood

One of the great truths that came from the so-called prison temple, Liberty Jail, had to do with priesthood and Church government. This is found in section 121 of the Doctrine and Covenants, a part of which reads as follows: "Behold, there are many called, but few are chosen. And why are they not chosen? Because their hearts are set so much upon the things of this world, and aspire to the honors of men, that they do not learn this one lesson—That the rights of the priesthood are insepara- bly connected with the powers of heaven, and that the powers of heaven cannot be controlled nor handled only upon the principles of righteousness." (D&C 121:34-36.)

On one occasion the Prophet Joseph Smith was asked how he governed his people. His reply was, "I teach them correct principles and they govern themselves." (Quoted by John Taylor, *Journal of Discourses* 10:57-58.) The doctrine of righ- teous dominion, so beautifully described in section 121, is a good example of how members of the Church are taught correct principles that enable them to govern themselves.

We believe that one of the important purposes of this life is to be proved, tried, and tested. Both the Zion's Camp and the Liberty Jail experiences truly constitute a refiner's fire for those who participated in them; they emphasize the necessity of ex- periencing difficult and complex situations in life in order to properly develop and draw close to our Heavenly Father.

Two Lessons for Us

What can we learn from Zion's Camp and Liberty Jail that will help us?

Certainly two impressive truths are apparent: first, the importance of faith in the Lord Jesus Christ and loyalty to our leaders and the Church, and second, the need of enduring to the end regardless of how many difficulties we have to surmount.

In order to apply these principles in our lives, let us today commit ourselves to follow the counsel of our leaders, accept every opportunity to serve, and complete each assignment well—yes, endure to the end. Let us avoid setting our hearts upon the things of the world; as we exercise our priesthood, let us incorporate the great principle of righteous dominion. By so doing and by keeping the commandments of the Lord, we shall have joy, happiness, growth, and development, and "eternal life, which gift is the greatest of all the gifts of God." (D&C 14:7.)

Prepare for Adversity

We should not expect that everyone will speak well of us, or that all will be well with us continually. Let us prepare to face adversity steadfastly regardless of the form it takes, recognizing that such experiences are necessary to the progress of the Church as well as to ourselves as individuals.

God has not promised that we won't have problems and troubles; but He has promised us comfort, increased faith, and knowledge, as well as growth and development, as we successfully meet each challenge of life. What may appear to be a small problem to some may be a major one to another. The important thing about a problem is how we react to it.

The Promised Blessing

I can promise you that as you do your part, the Lord will make you equal to every task that you are called upon to perform. As you develop the spirit of giving and sharing and of solving your problems, you will find peace, happiness, joy, and contentment, as well as growth and development.

May I encourage you, therefore, to accept every opportunity presented to you with enthusiasm—not as a burden, but as a blessing. Organize your time by putting first things first, and perform each assignment well. By so doing, the divine spark within you will be magnified and your talents will be increased, "yea, even an hundred fold." (D&C 82:18.)

Church Expansion

The Gospel Shall Roll Forth

In a revelation given to the Prophet Joseph Smith, the Lord revealed that "the keys of the kingdom of God are committed unto man on the earth, and from thence shall the gospel roll forth unto the ends of the earth, as the stone which is cut out of the mountain without hands shall roll forth, until it has filled the whole earth. . . . Wherefore, may the kingdom of God go forth, that the kingdom of heaven may come." (D&C 65:2, 6.)

Our mission is here defined as being worldwide as we prepare for the coming of our Lord and Savior Jesus Christ; and in fulfilling our mission, the Church is fast becoming a worldwide organization.

George Albert Smith's Challenge

In 1947, as the Saints were celebrating the one hundredth anniversary of the entrance of the Mormon pioneers into the Salt Lake Valley, President George Albert Smith addressed a communication to the members of the Church, entitled "Looking Ahead—into a New Century of Growth and Development." In this article he stated: "I assure every man and woman of the Church that you have a great obligation to spread the word of the Lord abroad and to carry the truth to every land and clime so that the power of the Priesthood will be made manifest among our Father's children in many places where it has never yet even been heard of. . . .

"That is the spirit of the Gospel of Jesus Christ. Great is the joy that comes into the hearts of the men and women who devote themselves to doing what our Heavenly Father desires of them, and great will be their happiness as they participate in the new era of growth and development that lies ahead for the Church as we look forward into a new century of progress." (*Church News*, December 20, 1947, p. 1.)

Knowledge Explosion

Anthropologists tell us that if we were to construct an imaginary graph of the growth of human knowledge, the bar representing everything man knew up to the steam age would be three inches high. A second bar, representing the gain in knowledge from the steam engine to the atomic bomb, would be fifteen inches high. But a third bar, representing the knowledge gained from the atomic age to the present, would have to be higher than the Washington Monument! This powerful illustration points up the rapidity of change in our time.

The Spirit of the Lord is truly being poured out upon the face of the earth. This is in fulfillment of prophecy. Since 1947, tremendous changes have occurred in transportation, communications, electronics, and in many other areas.

The Church has been quick to utilize the jet airplane, television, radio, shortwave broadcasting, and electronic equipment in building a worldwide organization. True, the basic principles of the gospel are eternal and do not change. However, the methods used in bringing the gospel to the attention of God's children and administering the affairs of the Church on a worldwide basis must be geared to the age in which we live.

Our Opportunities Today

Today, as a worldwide church, The Church of Jesus Christ of Latter-day Saints has a tremendous appeal to young and old alike because it is a dynamic yet realistic plan of life. It offers involvement and expression for all. When you stop to consider, every program of the Church is aimed at the development of character and leadership.

Despite the fact that we are living in a troublesome period, we are living in the dispensation of the fulness of times, a most wonderful period in the history of the world, yes, in a new era of growth and development. Opportunities today, for young and old, exceed those of any other age.

President Spencer W. Kimball has asked us to lengthen our stride in building the kingdom. Lengthening our stride certainly must include being more effective in our Church responsibilities.

Applying the "Beehive Spirit"

Utah is known as the Beehive State. The early settlers, under the leadership of Brigham Young, named the area Deseret, meaning "the honey bee." Therefore, the state motto is "Industry." However, the beehive represents more than industry. It also suggests swarming and the making of more colonies of bees. This means the gathering of more honey to feed more bees and thus extend more blessings. In the pioneer days of Brigham Young, the swarming of new converts was to the Rocky Mountain area. Although there was only one Brigham Young, all pioneers became a part of the pioneering effort— may I say, "the swarming program"?

But what about this new era of growth and development? President Kimball has said that "pioneering is the American way." The beehive spirit of industry and swarming is just as applicable today as in the days of Brigham Young, except that our

opportunities today include worldwide swarming—the building of the Church in many parts of the world. Today the new
members or colonies are requested to stay in their own lands
and swarm there.

As the leaders of the Church in recent years have emphasized the advisability of building up strong units of the
Church throughout the world, many interesting things are
happening. The number of full-time missionaries has increased, as has the number of missions. And as a part of today's
pioneering program, President Kimball has requested that the
stakes and missions furnish more of their own full-time missionaries. As these missionaries are called in many countries
throughout the world, they need financial help. Our assisting
them financially is another part of our present pioneering effort. We have the opportunity to make contributions as
quorums and as individuals to the International Missionary
Fund. In this way we, in effect, call our bank accounts on a mission. These missionaries become leaders of the Church in these
scattered areas of the world as they return from their missions.

Yes, satisfying pioneering opportunities are available today
as they were in 1847. Modern pioneering is a thrilling experience, and each of us can be a part of it in one way or another.

Decisions

The Parable of the Sower

Jesus did much of His teaching through the use of parables. In teaching in this manner, He used familiar illustrations, such as farmers, seeds, sowing weeds and thorns, harvests, shepherds, sheep and wolves, and many other illustrations familiar to those whom He was teaching. A beautiful example is the parable of the sower:

"Behold, a sower went forth to sow; and when he sowed, some seeds fell by the way side, and the fowls came and devoured them up: Some fell upon stony places, where they had not much earth; and forthwith they sprung up, because they had no deepness of earth: And when the sun was up, they were scorched; and because they had no root, they withered away. And some fell among thorns; and the thorns sprung up, and choked them: But other fell into good ground, and brought forth fruit, some an hundredfold, some sixtyfold, some thirtyfold." (Matt. 13:3-8.)

The sower had a choice to make—whether to prepare the soil for the seed or to take a chance and sow the seed without preparing the ground, hoping that the seed would fall on good ground. He was, however, careless, and he chose to take a chance, sowing without preparing the soil. Some seeds fell by the wayside and were eaten by the birds. Some fell among thorns and were choked out. He learned that sowing where birds ate and where the thorns choked was not profitable.

Had he prepared the soil before sowing, he might have reaped a hundredfold. This sower truly witnessed the truth of the statement that "whatsoever a man soweth, that shall he also reap." (Gal. 6:7.) The choice he made before sowing commenced determined to a large extent the harvest he was to reap.

Free Agency and Consequences

Each of us is in many respects in the same position as the sower. We each have free agency, or what we call the freedom of choice. When we sow without regard to the consequences, we reap sparingly. On the other hand, when we carefully observe the laws of progress and happiness, we reap growth, development, and happiness.

The law that says "whatsoever a man soweth, that shall he also reap," is also stated in other words, such as: "I, the Lord, am bound when ye do what I say; but when ye do not what I say, you have no promise." (D&C 82:10.) "There is a law, irrevocably decreed in heaven before the foundations of this world, upon which all blessings are predicated—and when we obtain any blessing from God, it is by obedience to that law upon which it is predicated." (D&C 130:20-21.)

The law of free agency indicates, in effect, that we may know the end of our lives from the beginning, and that to a considerable extent we can control the processes of life that bring us happiness and success or sorrow and failure. This law was given to Adam in the Garden of Eden. Moses gave the law of God to the children of Israel and promised them blessings for obeying and a penalty for disobedience. The prophet Joshua proclaimed, "Choose you this day whom ye will serve." (Josh. 24:15.) The Savior told His disciples, "For where your treasure is, there will your heart be also. . . . No man can serve two masters." (Matt. 6:21, 24.) We must choose which master to serve —God or Mammon, right or wrong. Let us select the right kind of seed and sow in well-prepared, fertile fields, where we can harvest a hundredfold.

Don't Live by Chance

I counsel you to make wise choices in everything you do. Avoid living by chance. Despite the great odds against them, many people actually leave much of their lives to chance. The selection of friends is many times left to chance. Yet the kinds of friends one has will often determine the kind of life one has. The selection of an occupation is frequently left to chance, with little or no effort being made to determine which line of work one is best suited for. Choose wisely, that you may reap a hundredfold. Do not leave the kinds of friends you have or your life's occupation to chance.

Many young people leave to chance the conditions leading up to marriage, which means that the success or failure of such a marriage is left to chance. Some leave their conversion to the gospel up to chance. By choosing a consistent course of religious education, one may know more about the gospel than otherwise and be better able to resist temptations.

Be Willing to Learn

The Lord has counseled us to study things out. This requires willingness to learn, a wise choice that has been a mark of greatness in every outstanding person. From the inception of the Church our leaders have chosen a wise course and have urged all members to improve their minds and to acquire knowledge as they go through life.

Brigham Young was a great advocate of learning. On one occasion he reportedly said, "This is our labor, our business, and our calling, to grow in grace and in knowledge from day to day and from year to year. We shall never see the time when we shall not need to be taught nor when there will not be an object to be gained."

In our Church activity, willingness to learn indicates true humility and a desire to accept counsel and advice. The Church has provided educational opportunities for all members, regardless of age, and we should humble ourselves and choose to learn from those assigned to teach us. Otherwise, we cannot progress.

Those who teach us should make certain their teachings are in harmony with the teachings of the Lord and are helpful to the growth and development of those being taught. The Lord has said that His work and His glory is "to bring to pass the immortality and eternal life of man." (Moses 1:39.) The Church has been established to assist in this matter. Every teacher in the Church, therefore, has the responsibility of building testimonies in the hearts and the minds of his students.

Great but Quiet Courage

In making choices and decisions, many times great courage is needed. In this respect, as in all others, the Savior gave us a perfect pattern of life. He said, "Be not afraid of them that kill the body, and after that have no more that they can do." (Luke 12:4.)

Christ's temptations and His victory over temptation set the pattern for each of us. As the Apostle Paul wrote to the Hebrews, "Though he were a Son, yet learned he obedience by the things which he suffered." (Heb. 5:8.) The Savior's courage was the quiet kind that we need in order to meet life's daily problems—the courage to carry life's burdens without complaining and to be honest with ourselves.

The Savior chose wisely. As we choose to develop this kind of courage by following gospel teachings, we can meet temptations and obstacles and not falter. We can meet adversity and disappointments, endure ingratitude and injustice, and never become discouraged.

The Lord Won't Make Our Decisions for Us

As we exercise our free agency and make wise choices, growth and development naturally occur. However, I think that many of us, even though we recognize these concepts, still want the Lord to make our decisions for us, or at least to inspire us without much effort on our part. In this respect, we must recognize that indecision itself is in reality a decision, and generally, in my opinion, a very poor one.

On one occasion Oliver Cowdery was attempting to translate and was not having much success. By way of a revelation given through the Prophet Joseph Smith, Oliver was told, "Behold, you have not understood; you have supposed that I would give it unto you, when you took no thought save it was to ask me. But, behold, I say unto you, that you must study it out in your mind; then you must ask me if it be right, and if it is right I will cause that your bosom shall burn within you; therefore, you shall feel that it is right. But if it be not right you shall have no such feelings, but you shall have a stupor of thought that shall cause you to forget the thing which is wrong." (D&C 9:7-9.)

So it is that many times we suppose that the Lord will make our decisions for us when we take no thought other than to ask Him. He tells us that the way to make wise decisions and choices is to study the matter out in our own minds, make the choice, and then, if we desire His help, we can ask Him if the choice we have made is right. If it is right, He will cause us to feel that it is right. But if it is a poor choice, we will have a stupor of thought and will not feel good about it.

When you make a choice, when you make up your mind to do something, I suggest that you then lay out a plan to accomplish it. After you have put your hand to the plow, do not look back. Have the courage to follow through with your decision as the Prophet counsels.

It is vital that we learn to make wise choices and control ourselves, rather than to live by chance. May we also develop courage to execute these wise choices we make from day to day.

Use Gospel Standards, Not Science or Philosophy

Let me suggest that we reexamine our standards of right and wrong and determine what standards are best for ourselves and for the common good of our fellowmen. I am convinced that neither science nor philosophy can satisfactorily answer important questions dealing with the purpose of life, but that the gospel of Jesus Christ can. The gospel of Jesus Christ is a plan of life and teaches that all men are children of God. It clearly sets our standards of right and wrong.

As we incorporate gospel principles or standards into our lives, we have the confidence and respect of our fellowmen, enjoy love and harmony in our family relationships, and are blessed with peace of mind. We are, indeed, living the good life.

Eternal Progression

The Most Valuable Possession

We are told to "seek . . . first the kingdom of God, and his righteousness" (Matt. 6:33), and as we do so, "all things shall be added according to that which is just" (D&C 11:23).

In a revelation to the Prophet Joseph Smith just prior to the organization of the Church, the Lord said, "Seek not for riches but for wisdom, and behold, the mysteries of God shall be unfolded unto you, and then shall you be made rich. Behold, he that hath eternal life is rich." (D&C 6:7.)

"If you keep my commandments and endure to the end you shall have eternal life, which gift is the greatest of all the gifts of God." (D&C 14:7.)

Recognizing, then, that the greatest eternal value is eternal life, let us consider what we are required to do on this earth to lay hold of this most desirable gift. In the scripture just quoted the Lord said that if we keep His commandments and endure to the end, we shall have eternal life. Eternal life involves eternal progression, and eternal progression requires the application of eternal principles or laws. *To progress is, in reality, more vital than being.*

We Need Wisdom

Let me consider with you a quality that must be developed to assure eternal progression—*intelligence.* The most familiar scripture with reference to this matter is found in the Doctrine and Covenants 93:36, where the Lord says, "The glory of God is intelligence, or, in other words, light and truth." And again the Lord said, "Whatever principle of intelligence we attain unto in this life, it will rise with us in the resurrection. And if a person gains more knowledge and intelligence in this life through his diligence and obedience than another, he will have so much the advantage in the world to come." (D&C 130:18-19.) These scriptures clearly state the great need to acquire knowledge in order to progress eternally and to gain eternal life.

The Prophet was counseled, "Seek ye diligently and teach one another words of wisdom; yea, seek ye out of the best books words of wisdom; seek learning, even by study and also by faith." (D&C 88:118.)

Vision is unusual foresight that improves one's judgment and assists greatly in setting realistic goals and objectives.

Discernment stresses accuracy in reading character and motives. It is also akin to perception, insight, and acumen—all of which are important qualities to develop. These qualities are extremely helpful in contributing to our eternal progress. They are likewise developed through experience and acquisition of intelligence.

Study the Gospel

We are told that "he that walketh with wise men shall be wise: but a companion of fools shall be destroyed." (Prov. 13:20.) A leader and a good church worker must possess knowledge and be knowledgeable about any matter that he desires to interest others in. Actually, one seldom becomes interested in anything until he acquires considerable knowledge concerning the matter. I therefore encourage you to study the gospel continuously and particularly to become familiar with subjects in areas of activity in which you must supervise, inspire, and motivate people. Knowledge combined with spirituality and faith will prepare a person to motivate, stimulate, encourage, strengthen, and inspire.

Feed Your Spirit

As we gain education, knowledge, and ability, let us remember it is just as important to feed and develop the spirit as it is to feed the mind and the body. A person might have a brilliant mind and an able and well-trained body, but if he has neglected building his faith and spirituality, he may do very little of real value.

One may lose his eyes, his hearing, or his voice, or all three, and still be useful and successful. One may lose his hands or his feet, or both, and still do useful work and be a credit to his family and his country. One may lose his health and suffer all his life and still be a great musician, a poet, an artist, or a statesman. No one has ever written sweeter music than Beethoven, who could not hear. No one perceived more clearly the beauties of nature than Milton, who could not see. Blind men have achieved fame as lawyers, senators, educators, and missionaries.

One can overcome almost any handicap when he retains his spirit. When his spirit falters, however, even though he may have a strong and perfect body, he will accomplish little. That which strengthens and ennobles the spirit of man improves society and carries the world forward toward its goal of better, finer, and more righteous living.

Poverty is no disgrace and scarcely a handicap to the courageous of spirit. When men develop their self-reliance by meeting and solving the problems that present themselves, they achieve great strength, integrity, and force of character. They demonstrate the fact that they are spirit children of God, the Eternal Father, and achieve the potential given them by their Father in heaven.

The Blessing of a Body

One of the outstanding blessings of this earth life is to obtain a body for our spirit to inhabit. Lucifer's great punishment was that he should not possess a body.

The Apostle Paul wrote to the Corinthian Saints: "Know ye not that ye are the temple of God, and that the Spirit of God dwelleth in you? If any man defile the temple of God, him shall God destroy; for the temple of God is holy, which temple ye are." (1 Cor. 3:16-17.)

Inasmuch as our body is the abode of our spirit, which is the offspring of God, we should make certain that we do not defile it. To this end the Lord has given us a specific Word of Wisdom by revelation. This principle was given with a promise, "adapted to the capacity of the weak and the weakest of all saints, who are or can be called saints." (D&C 89:3.) It contains a promise that "all saints who remember to keep and do these sayings . . . shall receive health in their navel and marrow to their bones; and shall find wisdom and great treasures of knowledge, even hidden treasures; and shall run and not be weary, and shall walk and not faint." (D&C 89:18-20.)

We are counseled to eat and drink foods and beverages that are beneficial to our bodies and to refrain from taking anything into our bodies that is injurious or harmful. We can likewise protect our health by getting proper exercise and rest.

The Word of Wisdom is a basic law, and those who live the law will be strengthened in body and in mind.

"The Weak and Simple"

During the early history of the Church, the Lord, in revelations to the Prophet Joseph Smith, explained that the fulness of His gospel would be restored and that it would be "proclaimed by the weak and the simple unto the ends of the world, and before kings and rulers" (D&C 1:23), but that He required "the heart and a willing mind," and that the Saints should "be not weary in well-doing" (D&C 64:34, 33).

"And inasmuch as they were humble they might be made strong, and blessed from on high, and receive knowledge from time to time," and they would "have power to lay the foundation of this church, and to bring it forth out of obscurity and out of darkness." (D&C 1:28, 30.)

In these revelations, the Lord explains His use of "weak and simple" instruments to proclaim His gospel. However, He gave the Saints commandments that they might possess understanding and knowledge, receive power, and become strong, thereby qualifying themselves to be effective servants.

The Prophet Joseph Smith is the chief example. He was weak insofar as the learning of men was concerned, but because he was humble, obedient, and had a willing mind, he became a strong and mighty leader and witness of the divinity of the Lord and Savior Jesus Christ.

In all ages this has been the pattern for those who would succeed in the work of the ministry: humility, prayer, dedication, and a desire and willingness to learn the will of the Lord. With the development and application of these qualities come knowledge, power, and strength.

Membership in The Church of Jesus Christ of Latter-day Saints provides many opportunities to participate in the building of the kingdom of God, and what a great privilege this is! We should, therefore, have an impelling desire to be humble and become strong that we might be worthy and able instruments—strong spiritually, morally, mentally, physically, financially, and in every way.

In these latter days, the Lord has reconfirmed that His Spirit "is sent forth into the world to enlighten the humble and contrite." (D&C 136:33.) This is the path to spiritual, moral, and mental power and strength.

Survival versus Unselfishness

So many times we hear people say: "What does this mean to me?" or "What do I get out of it?" This is frequently the first thought when a new suggestion is made.

The law of survival is so much with us that we often fail to look at a matter from the standpoint of others—or from the standpoint of what would be best for the majority. We claim to be Christians, but to what extent do we practice Christ's teachings? We hear certain phases of the gospel plan so frequently that we may live those teachings somewhat automatically. However, we sometimes overlook other important teachings that are not mentioned so often.

The Savior continually emphasized the doctrine of unselfishness. "Whosoever will be chief among you, let him be your servant." (Matt. 20:27.) He taught the rich young man to give generously and sacrifice all of his earthly goods, but the young man went away sorrowing. (Mark 10:17-22.) He illustrated his point in the beautiful story of the Good Samaritan. (Luke 10:30-37.) He taught forgiveness when the offender repented. To what extent? "Until seventy times seven!" (Matt. 18:22.)

Faith and Works

The Need for Faith

We are living in a period when one crisis follows another. Faith in mankind is being disturbed and destroyed. Men's hearts are troubled and seem to be failing them. There is a disposition even in Christian countries to rule out of life the mission of Jesus Christ.

However, the first statement in the declaration of belief of The Church of Jesus Christ of Latter-day Saints is: "We believe in God, the Eternal Father, and in His Son, Jesus Christ, and in the Holy Ghost." (Article of Faith 1.)

This belief in God is the life-giving element of the Church. To me it is one of the most interesting and inspiring principles to contemplate.

The Savior said, "Let not your heart be troubled: ye believe in God, believe also in me. . . . I am the way, the truth, and the life: no man cometh unto the Father, but by me." (John 14:1, 6.) The gospel of Jesus Christ is the plan of life that will restore peace to the world, remove inner tensions and troubles, and bring happiness and contentment. It is the greatest philosophy of life ever given to man.

Achieve the Impossible

Faith is the first principle of the gospel plan, and when coupled with works, it will bring success in one's school work, in one's home life, and in one's church and business activities. Faith makes it possible to accomplish what seems impossible to accomplish. As we study the life of the Prophet Joseph Smith, this is apparent in many of the things that he did.

Although Joseph Smith was persecuted and mocked, he developed great faith; he showed this in his testimony when he said, "I had seen a vision; I knew it, and I knew that God knew it, and I could not deny it." (Joseph Smith—History 1:25.)

Abraham Lincoln had high goals and great faith. It is reported that he said, "Poor and humble though I am, I have a chance. In my country no doors are barred to me because I am poor. I can work. Be the reward much or little, it will be mine. I can learn; the knowledge will give me power. Thank God I have a chance. Let us have faith that right makes might, and in that faith, let us to the end dare to do our duty, as we understand it."

Faith in Aspirin

It is in the period of youth that ideals grow brightest. We cannot get away from ideals and goals; and when we do not choose high ideals and goals, low ones choose us. It has been said that some of us have more faith in an aspirin pill than in God. Why do we have faith in an aspirin pill? Because we have seen it relieve pain. Yet every day of our lives we see the results of faith in God, including happiness, achievement, love, health, growth, and development.

Faith Starts in the Mind

How do you develop faith? First you have to make up your mind. Our mind is one of the most important parts of our body, the center of all our decisions. We have the right to choose good or evil. The decision is made in our mind. When you really make up your mind to be successful in anything in life, ninety percent of your problem is solved; the other ten percent has to do with things that you must do to accomplish your objectives.

Faith without works is dead. But faith with works will perform miracles. What do I mean by miracles? Things that seem impossible to accomplish. How do you accomplish these things? You think about a problem, you decide on a plan, you exercise courage, and you set about to accomplish your objective. And when you do your part, what does the Lord do? He magnifies you. He makes you equal to the task. He gives you wisdom, understanding, judgment, and discernment far beyond your ordinary capacity. Now these things happen, but we have to do our part first.

You can develop faith by realizing that there are two influences in the world; one is positive, and the other is negative. Everything that is good and positive, that will develop growth, that will bring you happiness, joy, health, and peace comes from the Lord. Everything that will tear you down, such as negative thoughts, concerns, fears, laziness, and doubts, comes from the evil one.

Faith and Works

In considering faith, we should recognize that it does not promise something for nothing. The apostle James asked the question, "What doth it profit, my brethren, though a man say he hath faith, and have not works? can faith save him? If a brother or sister be naked, and destitute of daily food, and one of you say unto them, Depart in peace, be ye warmed and filled; notwithstanding ye give them not those things which are needful to the body; what doth it profit? Even so faith, if it hath not works, is dead, being alone." (James 2:14-17.)

The Prophet Joseph, in speaking on this subject, said: "Let us here observe, that a religion that does not require the sacrifice of all things never has power sufficient to produce the faith necessary unto life and salvation . . . and it is through the medium of the sacrifice of all earthly things that men do actually know that they are doing the things that are well pleasing in the sight of God." "And as faith is the moving cause of all action in temporal concerns, so it is in spiritual." (*Lectures on Faith* 6:7; 1:12.)

Gospel of Work

Frequently we refer to the gospel of Jesus Christ as the gospel of work. The Prophet Joseph stated in his *Lectures on Faith* that this means mental as well as physical effort. (*Lectures on Faith* 1:10.) Plans must be carefully developed before important projects are commenced. All worthwhile endeavors require mental exertion—the making up of one's mind—before physical exertion comes into play.

We should realize that as we develop faith in the Lord Jesus Christ, it is possible and natural for us to develop faith in ourselves; and recognizing the importance of faith in our lives, we see the need of continually building our faith. Among other things, the building of faith involves prayerful study of eternal gospel principles, and the obtaining of a testimony involves making up one's mind to live the gospel and serve one's fellowmen through the sacrifice of earthly things. The Church of Jesus Christ of Latter-day Saints offers great opportunities for the building of faith.

What Is Faith?

Faith is necessary to accomplish anything of real value, but what is faith?

In his treatise on "True Faith," Orson Pratt said, "This is not an abstract principle, separate and distinct from mind, but it is a certain condition or state of mind itself."

In his *Lectures on Faith* the Prophet Joseph said, "We ask, then, what are we to understand by a man's working by faith? We answer—we understand that when a man works by faith he works by mental exertion instead of physical force. It is by words, instead of exerting his physical powers, with which every being works when he works by faith. . . . Faith, then, works by words; and with these its mightiest works have been, and will be, performed." (*Lectures on Faith* 7:3.)

Effective faith requires mental exertion, and we must, therefore, learn to think straight.

President Henry D. Moyle told some missionaries in Great Britain, "We can go out into the mission field; we can go into the world; we can go into our lives and accomplish anything that we desire to accomplish. Whenever the Lord calls upon us to do anything, he makes us equal to the task. The Lord bless us and give us the faith, and the determination, and the courage. I love these words." (Cited in *Autobiography of Franklin D. Richards* [Salt Lake City, 1974], p. 120.)

Recalling Orson Pratt's statement that faith is a condition or state of mind and President Moyle's statement that we can accomplish anything we desire to accomplish, it appears that our state of mind must be a positive or affirmative attitude rather than a negative attitude, and we must truly be enthusiastic. The word *enthusiasm* comes from a Greek word meaning "God in us." When we are enthusiastic about something, we want to share our joy with others.

Meet Life with Assurance

Prayer and study are important factors in building faith, and we should make these a part of each day's activities. Our faith will grow as we learn what our Father in heaven expects of us and as we do these things. Then as we keep in tune with his Spirit, we meet life's problems with the assurance that we will be successful and happy.

With increased faith we begin to recognize that we possess

to some degree many of the characteristics of our leaders, and we appreciate more and more that our Heavenly Father makes us equal to every responsibility that we are given. Yes, the faith of our leaders is a great inspiration to each of us.

Perseverance and Endurance

Now, a few thoughts concerning a characteristic that is so essential in growth and development: enduring to the end. When we speak of enduring to the end, I think we might ask, "To the end of what?" Can we endure to the end of a day with the same enthusiasm we had at the beginning of the day? Can we endure to the end of any assignment that we might receive, or do we give up the first time something goes wrong?

Each year has 365 days—each day is divided into periods — and each requires enduring to the end. Yes, enduring to the end requires endless enduring.

President Calvin Coolidge is reported as having said, "Nothing in the world can take the place of persistence. Talent will not—nothing is more common than unsuccessful men with talent. Genius will not—the world is full of educated derelicts. Persistence and determination alone are omnipotent. The slogan 'Press On' has solved and always will solve the problems of the human race."

Truly, persistence is a synonym for enduring to the end.

We sometimes refer to a person as a failure, but when is a person a failure? Is he a failure when his business fails or when he stumbles in his efforts? Is he a failure when he makes a mistake or when his goals are not realized? These do not make a person a failure. A person is a failure only when he quits, when he lacks persistence, when he contents himself to live at less than his best.

Enduring to the end means unswerving loyalty to one's family, friends, church, and country. Enduring to the end means everlasting honesty with ourselves, with our fellowmen, and with God. Enduring to the end means a continuing willingness to forgive those who trespass against us—not seven times but seventy times seven.

Enduring to the end means to be obedient to the laws of God eternally and to be willing to accept and live the laws and keep the ordinances of the gospel in this earth. Enduring to the end means to always serve our fellowmen in every way possible. Last and above all, enduring to the end means an everlasting, unfeigned love of the Lord and of our neighbors as ourselves.

Faith and Diligence

As he was concluding a great address to his people, King Benjamin said, "It is not requisite that a man should run faster than he has strength. . . . It is expedient that he should be *diligent,* that thereby he might win the prize; therefore, all things must be done in order." (Mosiah 4:27. Italics added.)

In this dispensation, through the Prophet Joseph Smith, the Lord has told us that every man should "learn his duty, and . . . act in the office in which he is appointed, in all *diligence.*" (D&C 107:99. Italics added.) Being diligent requires faith in the Lord Jesus Christ and in ourselves. Even though our assignments may seem difficult, as we develop our faith and persevere, we are able to achieve our righteous objectives.

Examples of Faith

You will recall that when Nephi was asked to return to Jerusalem and secure the records of his forefathers, he recognized the difficulties that would confront him. When his brothers were approached by their father, Lehi, they responded that it was a difficult thing that they were being asked to do, and they murmured against their father and his request. Nephi, on the other hand, did not murmur, although I am certain he recognized how difficult the task might be. He responded affirmatively, "I will go." (See 1 Ne. 3:1-7.)

On one occasion the Prophet Joseph Smith, in discussing his attitude toward doing the things that the Lord requests, made this statement: "I made this my rule: *When the Lord commands, do it.*" (*History of the Church* 2:170.)

I know that if a person will follow the examples of Nephi and Joseph Smith, he will develop more faith in the Lord Jesus Christ and in himself. He will find he can do the difficult things he is asked to do as he develops faith.

The Pay-offs for Having Faith

As a mission president, I emphasized to the missionaries the necessity of their developing faith, determination, and courage. How successful I was is illustrated in the case of Elder Smith. Sister Richards and I met Elder Smith six years after he was released from his mission, and he told us the following story.

He was seeking employment in a stock brokerage firm in Salt Lake City, and after being interviewed there, he was sent to the company's headquarters in San Francisco. In San Francisco two persons interviewed him, a young man and an older man with a cigar in his mouth. The older man, who seemed to be the one with the authority, told Elder Smith he understood that he had been on a mission for the Mormon Church. Elder Smith said he had. The man then asked, "What kind of missionary were you?" Elder Smith answered, "The best missionary in the mission." The man was so startled by this forthright answer that he almost dropped his cigar. He said, "If you were the best missionary in the mission, you are hired right now."

On one occasion at a district conference I was interviewing a man for his ordination to the office of elder. He was having some difficulty with the Word of Wisdom. I asked him what his attitude was, and he replied that there was nothing in the world that he would rather do than stop smoking. I told him that all he had to do was make up his mind never to have another cigarette. When he did that, I said, ninety percent of his problem would be solved; I would then tell him what the other ten percent was.

I asked him to make up his mind immediately—to look me in the eye, shake my hand firmly, and tell me that he would never have another cigarette. Then I extended my hand to him and asked him if he were ready. He hesitated a moment and then said no, he was afraid that if he promised he would not smoke and then later did, his conscience would hurt him.

Under these circumstances, I could not approve his ordination and told him so, as I felt there would be many things that he would not do that an elder should do. He left considerably disturbed. Later in the day, he asked to speak to me again. As he sat down, his eyes lit up. He said that he had made up his mind to stop smoking and that he had never experienced such a wonderful feeling in his whole life. He felt as though a fifty-pound weight had been lifted from his shoulders. He then asked me what the other ten percent was. I told him that if he had any cigarettes on him or at home, he was to immediately get rid of them so they would not be a temptation. I also suggested that he discontinue going out with his smoking friends on breaks. These and other things he could do to strengthen himself constituted the other ten percent. Then, with prayer and fasting by himself and with his family, he could be assured that the Lord would make him equal to the task of overcoming the smoking habit.

This incident occurred many years ago. The man has never smoked since, and he later became an honored and respected bishop. Thus, through his affirmative attitude and works, he manifested his faith; and with the help of the Lord, he achieved his goal.

Effective faith is always connected with works, and it is only through this combination that we achieve. This is indeed the key to success, happiness, and growth.

Blessings of Faith

Faith is a gift of God. Some of the blessings that come from obedience to the great principle of faith are: a desire to achieve worthwhile objectives, an affirmative attitude with the capacity to really make up one's mind, confidence and power that make the difficult or seemingly hopeless possible to attain, loyalty and steadfastness in service to our fellowmen, and, finally, peace and happiness resulting from achievement of worthwhile objectives.

Happiness in this world to a very large extent depends on the work a person does and the way in which he does it. It was necessary for each of us as spirits to leave the spirit world and come to this earth and learn to walk by faith, that the purposes of this life might be accomplished.

As we enter into each activity of life, both spiritual and temporal, let us apply these great fundamental and eternal principles of faith and works. By so doing, we can be assured, like Nephi of old, that the Lord will prepare a way for us to do the things we are assigned to do. Our hearts will not fail us, we will achieve our righteous objectives, and we will have that peace "which passeth all understanding." (Philip. 4:7.)

Genealogy

Creation of the Genealogical Society

In 1894, the Lord revealed to President Wilford Woodruff that it was necessary to have children sealed to their parents and the parents to their parents in all generations. The Saints were instructed to trace their genealogies back as far as possible. This would require many books and records and skilled workers. (See *Discourses of Wilford Woodruff* [Bookcraft, 1946], pp. 154-57.)

The Genealogical Society was organized, as a result, to collect, compile, establish, and maintain a library for the use of its members and others. The society is educational in disseminating information regarding genealogical matters, religious in acquiring records of deceased persons in connection with ordinances of The Church of Jesus Christ of Latter-day Saints. Today we undoubtedly have the most complete genealogical library in the world.

Becoming Converted to Genealogy

I agree with the statement contained in the priesthood correlation manual for the priesthood genealogical program that "there is a great difference between privilege and duty. In the past we have gone to great lengths in talking to our people about their duties and obligations with respect to genealogical work and their kindred dead. However, no amount of urging will bring success until people are first convinced and then converted to the need for such activity. . . . When our Church members are converted to the divine nature of the family relationship, they will do genealogical work." (*Priesthood Correlation in the Genealogy Program*, 1964, p. 4.)

Again quoting from the genealogical priesthood manual, "As one reviews these lofty thoughts, one is left to ponder the importance of priesthood genealogical work. It is not just searching for one's ancestry. It is not just a hobby or an interesting pastime. It is a spiritual work—the work of the salvation of both the living and the dead. It is the university level of spiritual activity in the Church which requires the best thought, the keenest minds and the greatest devotion to be found in the Church. Priesthood genealogy and temple work is a basic principle of priesthood activity and is the foundation upon which our eternal future rests." (Ibid., p. 8.)

After a person has received a partial vision of the work, he should actually do genealogical and temple work rather than just study. He can begin by filling in a pedigree sheet and a family group sheet of his own. The most difficult work is to fill out the first sheet. Once he has started, others will help him. But to catch the real spirit of genealogical work, one must go to the temple.

A Mission Like the Savior's

Our Savior, because of his great love for all of us, laid down His life that He might overcome death and make it possible for all of us to live again. We could not do this for ourselves; it could be accomplished only through his sacrifice.

Brigham Young said, "We have a work to do just as important in its sphere as the Savior's work was in its sphere. Our fathers cannot be made perfect without us; we cannot be made perfect without them. They have done their work and now sleep. We are now called upon to do ours; which is to be the greatest work man ever performed on the earth." (*Discourses of Brigham Young* [Deseret Book, 1954], p. 406.)

This Dispensation's Blessings

We can all be grateful that our spirits were reserved to come forth at this wonderful time and that we can bear witness that God lives and that Jesus is the Christ. May we appreciate our opportunities and responsibilities and develop the capacity to motivate and inspire God's children to accept their great opportunities and challenges in genealogical work.

The Holy Ghost

A Sign of the True Church

On one occasion the Prophet Joseph Smith, describing the differences between The Church of Jesus Christ of Latter-day Saints and other churches, said that one of the main differences was in our mode of baptism, including "the gift of the Holy Ghost by the laying on of hands"—that we believe in the continuing power of the Holy Ghost.

The first and fourth Articles of Faith outline this belief:

"We believe in God, the Eternal Father, and in His Son, Jesus Christ, and in the Holy Ghost."

"We believe that the first principles and ordinances of the Gospel are: first, Faith in the Lord Jesus Christ; second, Repentance; third, Baptism by immersion for the remission of sins; fourth, Laying on of hands for the gift of the Holy Ghost."

Through modern revelation we are told that "the Father has a body of flesh and bones as tangible as man's; the Son also; but the Holy Ghost has not a body of flesh and bones, but is a personage of Spirit. Were it not so, the Holy Ghost could not dwell in us." (D&C 130:22.) This is the simple and beautiful conception of the Godhead as taught by The Church of Jesus Christ of Latter-day Saints.

Effects of Rebirth

When Nicodemus, a ruler of the Jews, came to Jesus at night and asked him what he should do to be saved, he was told, "Except a man be born of water and of the Spirit, he cannot enter into the kingdom of God." (John 3:5.)

In this dispensation we have been admonished to "go among this people, and say unto them, . . . Repent and be baptized in the name of Jesus Christ, . . . for the remission of sins; and whoso doeth this shall receive the gift of the Holy Ghost, by the laying on of the hands of the elders of the church." (D&C 49:11-14.)

That this new birth included a spiritual regeneration was indicated when the Savior explained, "That which is born of the flesh is flesh; and that which is born of the Spirit is spirit. Marvel not that I said unto thee, Ye must be born again." (John 3:6-7.)

Faith in the Lord Jesus Christ, repentance, and baptism by water are prerequisites to receiving the Holy Ghost.

Cleanliness a Prerequisite

The Apostle Paul, in writing to the Corinthian saints, stated: "Know ye not that your body is the temple of the Holy Ghost which is in you?" (1 Cor. 6:19), and "If any man defile the temple of God, him shall God destroy, for the temple of God is holy, which temple ye are" (1 Cor. 3:17). To keep in tune with the Holy Ghost, we must keep our bodies clean in every respect.

President Brigham Young stated, "The Holy Ghost . . . opens the vision of the mind, unlocks the treasures of wisdom, and they begin to understand the things of God. . . . They comprehend themselves and the great object of their existence." (Journal of Discourses 1:241.)

If a person is going to get the most out of this life, he must comprehend the object of his existence. To worthy recipients, the gifts of the Holy Ghost are many, and extremely helpful in answering the question "What is the purpose of life or the object of our existence?"

A Witness and a Comforter

One of the chief functions of the Holy Ghost is to bear witness of God the Father and Jesus Christ, His Son. The Apostle Paul, in writing to the Corinthian saints, told them that "no man can say that Jesus is the Lord, but by the Holy Ghost." (1 Cor. 12:3.) To know that God lives and that Jesus Christ is His Son and our Savior and Redeemer is essential if we would understand the purpose of life.

In addition to being a witness for the Father and the Son, the Holy Ghost is a comforter. As the Savior was about to be crucified, He promised the disciples, "The Comforter, which is the Holy Ghost, whom the Father will send in my name, he shall teach you all things, and bring all things to your remembrance, whatsoever I have said unto you." (John 14:26.)

Thus we see that the Holy Ghost is a witness of the Father and the Son and a comforter. The Holy Ghost is also a teacher and the bearer of valuable gifts of the Spirit, such as wisdom, knowledge, faith, discernment, and direction.

A Cadet's Testimony

I recall a testimony given by a young cadet attending the United States Air Force Academy. He was experiencing great difficulty in passing his courses and was very discouraged. At this time, he met a Mormon cadet, and from him he learned that a number of Mormon boys were attending the academy and that they met together at five o'clock each weekday morning in a religious study class. The cadet was invited to attend one of these classes. He did so, and he was deeply impressed by the wonderful spirit. He continued attending, met the missionaries, was given the discussions, and, through study, prayer, and attending church, received a testimony and was baptized.

He bore witness that upon receiving the Holy Ghost, he felt its influence quicken his mind and understanding and refresh his memory. His feelings of discouragement left him, and a spirit of peace and comfort came over him, and thereafter he had no trouble in getting satisfactory grades. This was a most inspiring and impressive testimony of the value of the Holy Ghost.

Heeding the Spirit

When our children were young and we were living in Salt Lake City, I was presented with an opportunity to accept a government position in Washington, D.C. This was an important decision for our family to make. After careful and prayerful consideration, we decided to accept. We felt good about this decision, but it took considerable courage to follow the inspiration.

Years later, when I left government service, I had another important decision to make—whether to accept an attractive opportunity to work for others or go into business for myself. There were many pressures, many considerations, and after much deliberation, I decided to go into business for myself. After fervent prayer I felt strongly that this was the path to pursue. I prayed for the courage to follow the whisperings of the Spirit.

We hear many testimonies in which worthy members tell of having been warned of impending dangers. A young father bore witness to me of a great blessing that had come to him and his family. He was awakened one night by a voice that clearly told him to get up and go downstairs. He heeded the warning, and when he went into the kitchen, he found one wall engulfed in flames. Hurriedly he awakened his family, called the fire department, and, with the help of his family, fought the fire, keeping it down until the fire department arrived and put it out. There was no question in his mind that this warning was a manifestation of the protection the Holy Ghost can give to those who keep their lives in harmony with the Spirit.

Comfort in Times of Sorrow

The Savior has promised that the Holy Ghost will be a comforter to worthy members in times of sickness and death. Many have borne witness of the comforting spirit that has attended them in such times, helping them to find peace and understanding.

Some time ago I met two wonderful women, close friends, who had lost their husbands in a tragic airplane accident. Did I find them in despair and deep mourning? No, indeed. I have never witnessed greater courage and strength. They bore witness to the fact that they had truly felt the comfort of the Spirit, that they knew there was a purpose in the call that had been given to their husbands, and that they had an assurance that all would be well with them and their families as they lived close to the Church and kept the commandments of the Lord.

Feeling the Holy Ghost

Some time ago a young woman asked me, "How do you know when you are speaking under the influence of the Holy Ghost?" My answer was, "I can feel it spiritually and physically."

I have heard the still, small voice, or the whisperings of the Spirit, as I have counseled with the Saints, as I have conferred the priesthood upon men, as I have set men and women apart to positions in the Church, as I have given blessings to the sick, as I have borne my testimony to nonmembers as well as members, as I have been delivering sermons, and at many other times.

I bear my witness that as one accepts the restored gospel of Jesus Christ and conforms to the principles and ordinances thereof, the Holy Ghost will truly be a guide and comfort to him throughout his life.

Honesty

The Power of Honesty

As one forges a strong chain of life, the habit of honesty can well become one of the brightest and strongest links. There is great power in centering one's attention upon an ideal or principle like honesty. But in the minds of many, the real meaning of honesty, as a moral value, has been terribly twisted. Honest thinking and honest acting are desperately needed in today's society.

The dictionary defines honesty as the quality of being truthful, incorruptible, and free from deceit and fraud. In thinking of honesty, we may first think of our relations with others, but in many respects it is more important to be honest with ourselves. In the play *Hamlet,* Shakespeare has his character Polonius saying to his son Laertes, "This above all: to thine own self be true, and it must follow, as the night the day, thou canst not then be false to any man."

Each of us is endowed with the right to choose good or evil, and we should recognize that men do not succeed, nor are they destroyed, by other people or conditions, but rather by their own decisions.

Moral Cleanliness and Honesty

Honesty to one's own self embraces good health habits, good work and study habits, a determination to be of useful service to others, and, as the Apostle Paul says, an avoidance of rioting, drunkenness, "chambering," wantonness, strife, and envying. (Rom. 13:13.)

We recognize that our body is the temple of God and that the Spirit of God dwells in us, and with such knowledge, we should do everything possible to strengthen our bodies. This means avoiding the use of tobacco, liquor, tea, coffee, harmful drugs, and anything that harms or defiles the body.

Likewise, good thoughts that assist one to grow and develop and to be of use and service to his fellowmen stimulate mental and physical health, whereas degrading thoughts built around obscenity, immorality, strife, stealing, cheating, and lying result in unhappiness and ultimate destruction.

To be honest with ourselves, we must adopt good mental and physical health habits as our standards; we know that good health of body and mind contributes to a rich and rewarding life, a clear conscience, and inner peace.

Good Work Habits and Honesty

Again, good work and study habits are of major importance in living an honest and rewarding life. There are some who contend that hard work isn't necessary today in order to be successful and happy, but this is not true. The gospel plan requires each of us to work out our own salvation, our own happiness, growth, and development.

Let me quote a part of a letter written by an anxious father to his son to emphasize this matter:

"My son, remember you have to work. Whether you handle a pick or wheelbarrow or a set of books, digging ditches or editing a newspaper, . . . or writing funny things, you must work. . . . The work gives you appetite for your meals; it lends solidity to your slumber; it gives you a perfect appreciation of a holiday. There are young men who do not work, but the country is not proud of them. It does not even know their names. . . . So find out what you want to be and do. Take off your coat and make dust in the world. The busier you are, the less harm you are apt to get into, the sweeter will be your sleep, the brighter your holidays, and the better satisfied the whole world will be with you." (Bob Burdette, "Make a Dust," *Leaves of Gold,* ed. Clyde Francis Lytle [Williamsport, Pa.: Coslett Publishing Co., 1948], p. 184.)

Good work habits include such qualities as dependability, loyalty to employer, and willingness to go the extra mile, and finding happiness and purpose in your work.

Good Study Habits and Honesty

Now, concerning good study habits, let us consider why we read and study: to be informed, to gain wisdom and knowledge that will be of value to us, and to grow and develop. Yes, reading can become a most pleasant and profitable way to regularly spend a portion of our time—and especially reading of the scriptures.

Alfred C. Fuller, the founder of the Fuller Brush Company, said concerning his study of the Bible, "What most impresses me, as I look backward, is the immense application I have made of Bible truths in my daily life. From lack of education, I relied on the Bible as my text book, in every conceivable problem that arose. Only when I deviated from this teaching did I fail. He who does not live daily in its guidance is foolish, for he is rejecting the greatest source of personal profit that exists in the world. The Bible is the best 'how-to-do-it' book ever compiled, and it covers every fundamental that anyone really needs to know."

Let us be honest with ourselves and get into the habit of reading and studying the Bible and the other standard works of the Church as a guide to a rich and rewarding life.

Don't Let the End Justify the Means

We should exert our best efforts to accomplish our righteous objectives, utilizing every legitimate means but not permitting ourselves to commit a wrong in our quest for the right. It is better to lose than to win in an unjust or dishonest cause.

What better thing can a person learn than honesty in doing his best, in learning the best things in life, in reading the best books, in mingling with the best people, in doing the best things?

In so doing we are seeking the success of the inner man and will find family harmony, more and better relatedness to God and our fellowmen, and inner ease instead of tension. Thus we will achieve our new frontier and goal of a rich and rewarding life.

Joseph Smith

The Vital Difference

Members of the Church are frequently asked, "What is the difference between The Church of Jesus Christ of Latter-day Saints and other churches?" There are many important and significant differences, but probably the most basic difference is stated in our ninth Article of Faith: "We believe all that God has revealed, all that He does now reveal, and we believe that He will yet reveal many great and important things pertaining to the Kingdom of God."

In short, we are what many people call a peculiar people because we believe in modern revelation through a prophet of God.

Joseph Smith's Great Question

In the year 1820, Joseph Smith, a boy of fourteen who was living in the state of New York, was interested in joining a church but was unable to determine which church was right. In his own words, he said:

"While I was laboring under the extreme difficulties caused by the contests of these parties of religionists, I was one day reading the Epistle of James, first chapter and fifth verse, which reads: *If any of you lack wisdom, let him ask of God, that giveth to all men liberally, and upbraideth not; and it shall be given him.*

"Never did any passage of scripture come with more power

to the heart of man than this did at this time to mine. It seemed to enter with great force into every feeling of my heart. . . .

"At length I came to the conclusion that I must either remain in darkness and confusion, or else I must do as James directs, that is, ask of God. I at length came to the determination to 'ask of God.'"

So in accordance with his determination to ask of God, Joseph Smith retired to a grove of trees near his home one beautiful spring morning in 1820 and knelt in prayer. As he was praying, he saw, over his head, a pillar of light, brighter than the sun, which descended gradually until it fell upon him. When the light rested upon him, he saw, standing above him, two personages whose brightness and glory defied all description. One of them called Joseph by name and said, *"This is My Beloved Son. Hear Him!"* (Joseph Smith—History 1:11-17.)

I bear witness in all solemnity that Joseph Smith did see God the Father and His Son, Jesus Christ. In fact, he could see them as clearly as we see one another. And he could see that his own body was created in the image and likeness of God. At that time the churches taught that God was only a spirit, that He had no body. So we learn from this great vision that Joseph Smith experienced that God the Father and His Son Jesus Christ have bodies.

Which Church to Join?

In the grove that day, Joseph Smith asked the Savior which of all the sects was right and which he should join. In a most startling manner, he received this response: "I was answered that I must join none of them, for they were all wrong; . . . [that] they teach for doctrines the commandments of men, having a form of godliness, but they deny the power thereof." (Joseph Smith—History 1:19.) This was a blanket indictment of all Christendom. It means that there had been a universal apostasy from God. This, however, is entirely consistent with the work Joseph was chosen to do.

Joseph Smith's vision of God is unexcelled in the history of God's relationship with man. With the exception of Stephen's vision of God (Acts 7), God the Father has remained in the background, the Jehovah of the Old Testament being the premortal spirit of Jesus Christ, the Son of God.

The importance of the dispensation was indicated by the Father's introducing the Son to Joseph. This vision constitutes the most glorious event to occur in the history of the world since Jesus lived on the earth, and fittingly opens the dispensation of the fulness of times, the dispensation in which all things are to be gathered together in one.

With the opening of the dispensation of the fulness of times, it was appropriate that a fulness of the knowledge of God should be revealed to the prophet who was to stand at the head of the dispensation.

Effects of the First Vision

It is difficult to comprehend all the far-reaching effects of that first vision of Joseph Smith, the first direct revelation in modern times. Consider what it did:

First, it clarified the concept of the Godhead. It revealed that God is not without body, parts, or passions. He appeared to Joseph Smith as a man. For centuries the scriptures have taught that man was created in the likeness of God. This being true, God is in form the same as man.

Second, it clarified the doctrine of the oneness of the Godhead. God the Father and His Son, Jesus Christ, appeared as two separate personages, as separate and distinct as any earthly father and son. It is clear that the oneness of the Godhead is a type of unity of mind and purpose.

Third, it showed clearly that revelation from God to man has not ceased. Christendom for centuries had taught that revelation had ceased and that God could not be expected to directly communicate with man.

Through the vision, Joseph learned that there had been a universal apostasy from the doctrines of the Church of Christ. Now a new dispensation opened up; a new witness for God had been established.

Subsequent to that first vision, the Lord, through the Prophet Joseph Smith, restored the priesthood, the authority to act in the name of God, and authorized and directed the reestablishment of His church on the earth.

Contributions of the Restoration

Joseph Smith was the instrument through which the gospel in its fulness was restored with its ancient and eternal truths. Let us consider some of his contributions in this respect.

New scripture includes the Book of Mormon, a history of God's dealings with His people in the Western Hemisphere and a new witness for Christ. The Doctrine and Covenants is a most important book containing revelation specifically for us. The Pearl of Great Price includes the book of Moses or visions of Moses; the book of Abraham, which was translated from papyrus by Joseph Smith; the writings of Joseph Smith and extracts from his history; and the Articles of Faith, outlining the beliefs and teachings of Christ.

This new scripture has brought increased knowledge regarding the purpose of life; where we came from, why we are here, and where we go after death; our relationship to God and our need to progress eternally; and how to live and obtain happiness, peace, and contentment.

And with all of this increased knowledge that we have obtained through modern revelation, the Church of Jesus Christ has been restored.

The Mission of Joseph Smith

The Lord, speaking of the Prophet Joseph Smith, said on April 26, 1838, "For behold, I will be with him, and I will sanctify him before the people; for unto him have I given the keys of this kingdom and ministry. Even so, Amen." (D&C 115:19.)

And on January 19, 1841, while the Saints were at Nauvoo, the Lord said, "I give unto you my servant Joseph to be a presiding elder over all my church, to be a translator, a revelator, a seer, and prophet." (D&C 124:125.)

Joseph Smith suffered death as Jesus Christ did, and he left apostles and prophets, as Jesus Christ did, to direct the Church.

Yes, Joseph Smith performed his mission well.

Justice and Mercy

The Scriptural Union of Justice and Mercy

In the beautiful Sermon on the Mount, the Savior referred to the principle of mercy when he said, "Blessed are the merciful: for they shall obtain mercy." (Matt. 5:7.) And a great Nephite prophet asked, "Do ye suppose that mercy can rob justice? I say unto you, Nay; not one whit. If so, God would cease to be God." (Alma 42:25.)

In the scriptures justice and mercy are frequently mentioned together, and the thought arises: Can one be just and merciful at the same time, and can justice and mercy be merged? If so, how can we incorporate these principles in our lives to enrich them and qualify ourselves to better meet today's challenges?

The Golden Rule

The prophet Micah wisely asked, "What doth the Lord require of thee, but to do justly, and to love mercy, and to walk humbly with thy God?" (Micah 6:8.) Examining Micah's words regarding justice, mercy, and walking humbly before God should make it easier for us to determine if the principles of justice and mercy can be merged and used effectively in our lives.

In order to "do justly," honesty, fairness, and patience must characterize our dealings with others. Jesus expressed it this way: "Therefore all things whatsoever ye would that men should do to you, do ye even so to them: for this is the law and the prophets." (Matt. 7:12.) The Golden Rule is in reality the basic principle of dealing justly with our fellowmen.

Justice and Love

To "do justly" becomes a matter of attitude—a desire to go beyond tolerating others, making an effort to love and appreciate people by serving them. Justice is deeply affected by the principle of love.

Jesus also taught: "Judge not, that ye be not judged. For with what judgment ye judge, ye shall be judged: and with what measure ye mete, it shall be measured to you again. And why beholdest thou the mote that is in thy brother's eye, but considerest not the beam that is in thine own eye? . . . Thou hypocrite, first cast out the beam out of thine own eye; and then shalt thou see clearly to cast out the mote out of thy brother's eye." (Matt. 7:1-5.)

In being just, one will not condemn, find fault, or gossip, as there is no salvation in being critical of another. We should recognize that generally we cannot judge the motives that prompt others' actions, and usually the more we understand their motives, the less we are prone to condemn. The Savior has urged us to desist from evil and to aggressively go forward and do good.

Today there are many frustrated, confused, and discouraged people in the world. To "do justly," we are challenged to give them courage, hope, and strength; praise them and help them to understand that God loves them and has provided a way for them to be happy and successful; share with them the things with which we are blessed in order to make their loads lighter.

Overcoming Fear

Too often fear rules over the lives of people, depriving them of blessings. Fear must be overcome. The Lord has said, "If ye are prepared ye shall not fear." (D&C 38:30.) I bear you my witness that as we live the gospel principles, we will build faith in the Lord Jesus Christ and confidence in ourselves. Thus will we overcome fear.

Mercy and Forgiveness

Now let us consider the second thing the Lord requires of us, according to Micah, namely, that we have mercy. The Savior said, "Blessed are the merciful: for they shall obtain mercy." (Matt. 5:7.) We should also be aware that the reverse is true—that if we are not merciful, we shall not obtain mercy.

Many times true mercy incorporates forgiveness. Mercy and forgiveness, to be effective, require patience and understanding on the part of the one forgiving.

The apostle Peter asked Jesus how many times he should forgive one who would sin against him. The Savior's reply was, in essence, that Peter should forgive indefinitely: "Until seventy times seven." (Matt. 18:21-22.) Then He clarified the matter by giving the parable of the Unmerciful Servant, in which a certain king demanded payment of a debt one of his servants owed him, amounting to ten thousand talents. The servant asked for his lord's patience until he could pay the debt, whereupon the king had compassion on the servant and "forgave him the debt."

Then the servant went to a fellow servant who owed him a hundred pence; and "took him by the throat, saying, Pay me that thou owest." Although the servant's debtor asked for leniency, the servant cast him into prison.

When the king heard of this, he called the unmerciful servant and said to him: "O thou wicked servant, I forgave thee all that debt, because thou desiredest me: Shouldest not thou also have had compassion on thy fellowservant, even as I had pity on thee?

"And his lord was wroth, and delivered him to the tormentors, till he should pay all that was due unto him. So likewise shall my heavenly Father do also unto you, if ye from your hearts forgive not every one his brother their trespasses." (Matt. 18:23-35.)

The Obligations of Mercy

Anyone receiving mercy is under obligation to the one extending it, whether it be man or God. This is the obligation of living the Golden Rule. And we cannot reserve our mercy only for those who we think are worthy of it. Remember: "Judge not, that ye be not judged." (Matt. 7:1.)

The Prophet Joseph Smith, in discussing this matter, on one occasion stated: "God does not look on sin with allowance, but when men have sinned, there must be allowance made for them. . . . The nearer we get to our heavenly Father, the more we are disposed to look with compassion on perishing souls. . . . If you would have God have mercy on you, have mercy on one another." (*History of the Church* 5:24.)

There can be no license for sin, but we are told that mercy, justice, and love should go hand in hand with reproof. The Lord's words are these: "Reproving betimes with sharpness, when moved upon by the Holy Ghost; and then showing forth afterwards an increase of love toward him whom thou hast reproved, lest he esteem thee to be his enemy; that he may know that thy faithfulness is stronger than the cords of death." (D&C 121:43-44.)

This is especially important for us to remember as we reprove our children when the necessity arises.

The Prodigal Son

One of the greatest examples of mercy is that described in the parable of the Prodigal Son, considered by many to be one of the most beautiful stories ever written. Here we are told of the return home of a wayward son, of the father's great joy, and of the feast that celebrated his return. We must never forget, however, that although the wayward son was received back into his family with rejoicing and love, it was to the faithful son that the father said, "Son, thou art ever with me, and all that I have is thine." (Luke 15:31.)

Here we have an excellent example of how a wise, humble father merged the principles of mercy and justice to the benefit of his family. And here we see that all persons are precious in the sight of God.

Humility

The third requirement of the Lord, as explained by Micah, is to "walk humbly" with God. This requires strong faith that God is a just and merciful God.

Alma, addressing himself to this subject, said: "The plan of mercy could not be brought about except an atonement should be made; therefore God himself atoneth for the sins of the world, to bring about the plan of mercy, to appease the demands of justice, that God might be a perfect, just God, and a merciful God also." (Alma 42:15.)

As an example, Peter, James, and John were humble fishermen until they became active in building the kingdom of God; then they became a powerful influence in the lives of men.

Sincere prayer and service in the Church help one to develop faith in the Lord Jesus Christ and confidence in himself.

To walk humbly with God, we must love God and be humble, meek, and obedient. By walking humbly with God, by identifying ourselves with the building of the kingdom, we obtain inner strength and peace from our Heavenly Father, are happy and successful, and enjoy personal growth and development.

After considering Micah's words regarding justice, mercy, and walking humbly before God, it is easier to see how justice can be merged with mercy and how these principles can be beneficially incorporated in our lives to qualify us to better meet today's challenges.

Leadership

Leadership and Opportunities to Serve

Our complex society is built upon organization—governmental, religious, and social. This organization constantly requires more and more leaders. As a consequence, emphasis is placed on the development of leaders. Leadership is always coupled with opportunities to serve.

Opportunity is defined as a fit time, a favorable juncture of circumstances, a good chance. Leadership is the directing force of a movement.

As the Church grows at a greatly accelerated rate, there is and will be a much greater need for leaders. Not only in the Church, but in every phase of life, there is a crying need for leaders. More opportunities await the young leaders of today than any generation before.

I invite you to accept the challenge to become a leader, to set this as a goal. I would caution you, however, to never set your goal for a particular position, but rather to prepare youself so that when the opportunity comes, you will be ready—and you can be sure opportunity will come when you are qualified.

Develop Your Talents

Our Heavenly Father has blessed each one of us with talents. He has told us so. Your talents may be different from those of your brother or sister or friend, but you have them. You must find out what they are and develop them, that they might bring joy and happiness unto the lives of others and unto your own life.

The Prophet Joseph Smith said, "Every man who has a calling to minister to the inhabitants of the world was ordained to that very purpose in the Grand Council of heaven before this world was." (*Teachings of the Prophet Joseph Smith*, p. 365.) In the preexistence, we had our free agency, and I am sure we accepted these callings that we have here on this earth. The Lord did not compel us to accept these callings, nor will he compel us to magnify them; but we must appreciate the importance and sacredness of our assignments.

Pay the Price to Succeed

Accept my challenge to be a leader, and commit yourself to be a leader; set goals, and be willing to pay the price.

W. H. Murray has written: "Until one is committed, there is hesitancy, the chance to draw back, always ineffectiveness. Concerning all acts of initiative (and creation), there is one elementary truth, the ignorance of which kills countless ideas and splendid plans: that the moment one definitely commits oneself, then Providence moves too." (*Everest—The West Ridge* [San Francisco: Thomas F. Hornbein/Sierra Club, 1966], p. 100.)

Yes, faith with a positive commitment and works will perform miracles of many kinds.

Make Up Your Mind to Be Successful

As you make up your mind to be successful, you will develop the attitude of success. The attitude of success is a quality of mind and of spirit that will give vigor and strength to everything you do. Be affirmative in your thinking and your speech. Avoid negative words and phrases, such as "If," "I hope," "I'll try," and "I'll do my best." Say instead, "I'll do it." Smile and look people in the eye. Shake hands firmly. Be affirmative in your thinking and your speech.

Emerson said, "What will you have? quoth God; pay for it and take it." I believe that. Each of us can accomplish anything that we really want if we are willing to pay the price of dedicated preparation, not only of the mind and the body, but also of the spirit. It takes courage and dedication and stick-to-itiveness, but it can be done.

Learn to Think

Do you believe that you can accomplish anything that you desire to accomplish? I do! But how? Effectiveness in faith requires mental exertion, and we must, therefore, learn to think and to think straight.

Henry Ford is certainly an example of one who possessed great faith and leadership ingenuity. He reportedly said, "An educated man is not one whose memory is trained to carry a few dates in history. He is one who can accomplish things. A man who cannot think is not an educated man, however many college degrees he may have acquired. Thinking is the hardest work anyone can do—which is probably the reason we have so few thinkers."

As an administrator in government, as an executive in business, as a mission president, and as a supervisor in Church activities, I have found it necessary and practical to set aside time to think or meditate. I suggest that you plan your time so that you can have a regular time—at least once a week—to meditate. How much time? Well, this depends on your specific stituation, but I would suggest at least one to three hours.

IBM, one of the largest and most successful U.S. corporations, adopted the motto "Think" and uses it throughout its whole organization. House organs and individual signs on desks and walls say "Think." IBM has recognized that thinking is the key to leadership ingenuity.

One of President Heber J. Grant's favorite sayings, a quotation from Emerson, was: "That which we persist in doing becomes easier for us to do: not that the nature of the thing itself is changed, but that our power to do is increased." Practice thinking and concentrating, and it will become easier to do, and more effective.

I recall that when I was studying law at the University of Utah, Dean Leary used to tell us that he didn't care whether we remembered the principles of law that he was teaching us, but he wanted us to learn how to think straight. To do this, we learned that it was necessary to get the facts before reaching conclusions. He also impressed upon us the necessity of analyzing the facts from all angles in order to make sound decisions.

Learn to Make Decisions

To develop leadership capability we must also learn to make wise decisions. The ninth section of the Doctrine and Covenants contains a revelation given to the Prophet Joseph Smith in which Oliver Cowdery was told to study his problem out in his own mind, reach a decision, and then ask the Lord if his decision was right. If it was right, the Lord would give him a burning of his bosom, or a good feeling; if it was wrong, he would receive a stupor of thought, or an unsatisfactory feeling. (See D&C 9:8-9.)

Don't be too busy to meditate, and when the answer comes, have the courage to follow the whisperings of the Spirit. This is essential to the development of leadership and the effective use of time.

Remember Who You Are

Always remember that we are spirit children of God and are endowed with dignity, worth, and special talents. This doctrine clearly defines our possibilities and should give us a real sense of dignity and worth.

In modern revelation, we are told that "the spirit and the body are the soul of man" (D&C 88:15) and that "to every man is given a gift by the spirit of God" (D&C 46:11). Being spirit children of God, we have been asked by our Savior to become perfect even as our Father in heaven is perfect. (See Matt. 5:48.) We know also that as man is, God once was; and as God is, man may become—by obedience to the laws and ordinances of the gospel.

To be real leaders, we must learn to lead, to set an example, to never ask others to do things we are unwilling to do ourselves, and to have faith in the Lord Jesus Christ and in ourselves.

Goals and Priorities

In order to develop leadership abilities, we must learn to plan and to use our time effectively. I believe firmly that work is essential to success in any activity, but I would like to emphasize the importance of *effective* work rather than just work.

In planning, we develop long- and short-term goals and a series of priorities. Our longest-term goal, of course, is eternal life, which means exaltation in the kingdom of God. Our short-term goals break down the long-term goals into years, weeks, or days, and sometimes even into hours. What are you going to do today? Make a schedule of your day's activities and write down your goals. As you accomplish a short-term or a long-term goal, you are happy. Joy comes through achievement.

In all phases of my personal experience, I have found it wise to survey large fields but cultivate small ones. In surveying large fields, one in effect makes a master plan, which he later develops in orderly stages. He sets up short-term and long-term goals. This is a sound way to build and to avoid disappointments that can result from overextending oneself.

Yes, planning encompasses vision and faith. It is vital to effective leadership and use of time. Time is an all-important factor in life, and the experiences of a lifetime have taught me the value of eliminating nonessentials and concentrating on doing the present job well.

Preparation

In the standard works of the Church and in the words of counsel given by our leaders, we are given the information that we need to adjust our lives and prepare ourselves so that no matter what may transpire, we will be prepared. Study of the scriptures develops leadership capacity and assists us in spiritual achievement. I counsel you to continue your education and learning process eternally. This is part of the price you pay to develop leadership ability.

The Church of Jesus Christ of Latter-day Saints has a tremendous appeal for young people because it is a dynamic, yet realistic, plan of life. Involvement and active participation are basic principles. Activities such as participation in religious services, dramatics, public speaking, and sports contribute to the development of leadership ability.

The Greatest Goal

The Lord has told us that "the glory of God is intelligence," and "whatever principle of intelligence we attain unto in this life, it will rise with us in the resurrection." (D&C 93:36;

130:18.) This understanding of life opens up the great concept of eternal progression, giving us the greatest goal anyone can conceive of—a great goal, yet a realistic and practical one as we gaze into eternity.

The scriptures repeatedly tell us to pray always. As we live close to the Lord and learn to pray always, the whisperings of the Spirit will be clear.

Develop Spiritual Power

Further, as we develop leadership qualities, we must also develop deep spiritual strength, which will result in great power. We cannot be effective by ourselves. We must get in tune with the Holy Ghost and keep in tune with the Holy Ghost.

In the Doctrine and Covenants, the Lord tells us about our responsibilities and how to develop this power: "Again I say, hearken ye elders of my church, whom I have appointed: Ye are not sent forth to be taught, but to teach the children of men the things which I have put into your hands by the *power* of my Spirit; and ye are to be taught from on high. Sanctify yourselves and ye shall be endowed with *power*, that ye may give even as I have spoken." (D&C 43:15-16. Italics added.)

We sanctify ourselves by living the principles of the gospel. As we do this and study the scriptures, we are told that the Lord will give us power to give even as He has spoken. When we can do this, we are able to motivate people to join the Church and to accept and magnify their callings. We who are members of The Church of Jesus Christ of Latter-day Saints have the Holy Ghost to quicken our minds and understanding and to magnify our wisdom, discernment, and judgment. We must live in such a way that we will be entitled to the whisperings of the Spirit and have the courage to follow the inspiration we receive.

Courage to Walk into the Unknown

Remember that the courage to walk into the unknown is the courage required of all human beings, and that success is a journey, not a destination.

Let me assure you that the maximum joys and satisfactions of life and the maximum material rewards as well will come almost automatically to those who best serve their fellowmen. Therefore, never turn down an opportunity to serve in the Church. Live the principles of the gospel, and follow the leaders of the Church. Tragedy comes as a result of disobedience to the commandments of God, but peace, happiness, and success follow obedience.

Love

Showing Love

On one occasion the Savior told His disciples, "Love your enemies, bless them that curse you, do good to them that hate you, and pray for them which despitefully use you, and persecute you." (Matt. 5:44.) In this manner of serving others, Jesus considers all men, regardless of who they are, as having divine possibilities.

We have to a considerable extent evidenced our love of the Lord by accepting our assignments. We evidence our love of our neighbors by the service we render to them. Love is involved in every doctrine and activity of the gospel of Jesus Christ. Love is based upon truth.

A Positive Force

Love is a positive force that impels action. It is the driving force in God's relationship with man, a great creative and sustaining power.

The apostle John in his Gospel records the Savior's words: "For God so loved the world, that he gave his only begotten Son, that whosoever believeth in him should not perish, but have everlasting life." (John 3:16.) And again, "A new commandment I give unto you, That ye love one another; as I have loved you, that ye also love one another. By this shall all men

know that ye are my disciples, if ye have love one to another."
(John 13:34-35.)

We must do more than love and adore the Lord. The supreme demand is to serve one's fellows. Such service becomes
the outer manifestation of love and devotion.

The Effects of Love

Throughout His ministry, the Savior repeatedly counseled
His followers to avoid lying, stealing, and other abominations,
and to embark on a positive program of binding up the wounds
of the brokenhearted. By making love a positive program, one
puts courage, sunshine, and joy into the lives of others. Comfort is given those who mourn and are weary.

The world is full of frustrated souls that are tired and discouraged. Through love we give them courage and we give
them hope. The apostle James said, "Pure religion and unde-
filed before God and the Father is this, To visit the fatherless
and widows in their affliction." (James 1:27.)

We hear much of the Golden Rule. The Savior, in the Sermon on the Mount, expressed it this way: "Therefore all things
whatsoever ye would that men should do to you, do ye even so
to them: for this is the law and the prophets." (Matt. 7:12.)

The Best Way to Show Love

We love those whom we serve, and the best way to show our
love for our neighbors is to give them the opportunity to learn
of the restoration of the gospel of Jesus Christ—to give them
the "pearl of great price," a gift of eternal value to them. Let us
follow the Prophet's advice, "every member a missionary."
Love and service to one's fellows is truly the beginning and end
of God's labor with man.

Love, Prayer, and Sanctification

Shortly after the Church was organized, the Lord told the elders: "Sanctify yourselves and ye shall be endowed with power, that ye may give even as I have spoken." (D&C 43:16.)

How do we sanctify ourselves? By keeping God's commandments. Let us quickly consider just two commandments that contribute to the development of spirituality.

In answering the question, "What shall I do to inherit eternal life?" the Savior declared, "Thou shalt love the Lord thy God with all thy heart, and with all thy soul, and with all thy strength, and with all thy mind; and thy neighbour as thyself." (Luke 10:27.) We evidence our love of God and of our neighbors as we serve them.

Prayer is another essential element. The Savior instructed his disciples to "pray always." (Luke 21:36.) In an atmosphere of peace and communion with God, spirituality is nurtured and developed.

Love and prayer are involved in every doctrine and activity of the gospel of Jesus Christ; they are strong influences in developing spirituality.

Love of Others

It is impossible for a man to love God with all of his heart, soul, and mind and not love his fellowmen. In other words, one cannot really keep the first great commandment without keeping the second, and vice versa. When a Christian truly loves God he loves his fellowmen, and when he loves his fellowmen he loves God.

The apostle John wrote, "If a man say, I love God, and hateth his brother, he is a liar: for he that loveth not his brother whom he hath seen, how can he love God whom he hath not seen?" (1 John 4:20.) Paul's epistle to the Corinthians likewise emphasizes this doctrine: "Though I speak with the tongues of men and of angels, and have not charity, I am become as sounding brass, or a tinkling cymbal. And though I have the gift of prophecy, and understand all mysteries, and all knowledge; and though I have all faith, so that I could remove mountains, and have not charity, I am nothing." (1 Cor. 13:1-2.) Truly, without charity, compassion, and love, we are nothing.

Neighborliness, a Part of Second Birth

Jesus told Nicodemus that no man can enter the kingdom of God without being born again. This means, as he explained, baptism by both water and the spirit. (See John 3:3-5.) This rebirth of the Spirit means giving up selfishness, being willing to live the Golden Rule, and having a contrite spirit. A person with a contrite spirit will not cheat or misrepresent. Neither will he lie or be unfriendly to his neighbor.

It is apparent that a person cannot be saved without living the second great commandment. He cannot receive God's commendation, "Well done, thou good and faithful servant: . . . enter thou into the joy of thy Lord" (Matt. 25:21), if he fails to love his neighbor as himself.

Christ's Love for Others

When Jesus was asked, "Who is my neighbor?" he gave the parable of the Good Samaritan. All persons were Jesus' neighbors—His apostles and disciples, good men and women, and sinners—yea, even the thief on the cross. He washed His apostles' feet; He loved His fellowmen; He fed the hungry—physically and spiritually; He healed the sick and raised them from the dead.

Who are our neighbors? All persons everywhere who need our assistance. And what does this mean to us? It means that the Church offers us many opportunities to serve our neighbors.

Love Based on Truth

Elder John A. Widtsoe, in speaking about love being based on truth, said: "Love is always founded in truth. It is organically a part of truth. Lies and deceit, or any other violation of the moral law, are proofs of love's absence. Love perishes in the midst of untruth. That is a simple test of the presence of love. Thus, the lover who falsifies to his loved one, or offers her any act contrary to truth, does not really love her.

"Further, love does not offend or hurt or injure the loved one. By that test any human venture, past and present, may be measured for its real value. Cruelty is as absent from love as north is from south, as truth is from untruth." (*An Understandable Religion* [Independence, Mo.: Zion's Printing & Publishing Co., 1944], p. 72.)

Loyalty

An Age of Opportunity and Obstacles

Despite the fact that we are living in a wonderful age, we are living in a troubled world with an abundance of problems. In reality, this is one of the great purposes of life, to meet challenges and obstacles and learn to overcome them. Meeting obstacles and learning to overcome them give us experience, and each experience should be for our good.

The Need for True Freedom

Today we hear much about the need to "tell things as they are," the need for honesty and consistency in living, and the need for greater freedom. Someone has said, "There are two freedoms: the false freedom, where one is free to do what he likes, and the true freedom, where one is free to do what he ought to do."

I think it is appropriate and timely that we discuss some things as they are and can be as well as consider the difference between loyalty and disloyalty as pertains to the true and false freedoms.

First, loyalty to true freedom embraces love, dedication, faith, allegiance, willingness to sacrifice, and many other qualities that contribute to achievement and happiness. Disloyalty to true freedom embraces betrayal, unfaithfulness, disaffection, sedition, infidelity, and other qualities that contribute to failure, destruction, and unhappiness.

Loyalty to false freedom can only bring delusion, counterfeit happiness, and eventual destruction. False freedom principles include such things as the abuse of one's body by the use of drugs, liquor, and tobacco, as well as sexual immorality. False freedom principles likewise include the spread of Communistic doctrine and protest by force.

True freedom can exist only in doing what is right, in being loyal—yes, in doing what we ought to do. Let me be more specific and identify some things we ought to do to enjoy true freedom. We should be loyal to self, to family, to friends, to employer, to country, and to church and God.

Loyalty to Self

Shakespeare gave some sage advice when he said, "This above all: to thine own self be true, / And it must follow, as the night the day, / Thou canst not then be false to any man." (*Hamlet*, 1, iii, 78-80.)

One is true and loyal to himself when he develops himself mentally, physically, and spiritually; when he develops a proper standard by which all decisions are made and unswervingly follows the standard; when he keeps his self-respect and the respect of others by being noble and consistent in his ideals, acts, words, and thoughts; and when he combines faith with works in serving his God and his fellowmen.

Loyalty to Family

Loyalty to one's family and friends is likewise basic and paramount. It indicates love and affection. President David O. McKay said that no other success can compensate for failure in the home.

The Church provides a family home evening program that gives the family an opportunity to understand the principle of loyalty and how to make it a part of their lives. As family home evenings are held, great blessings result: there will be love at home, obedience to parents will increase, and faith will develop in the hearts of the youth.

Family loyalty means for each member to support and sustain every other member. Loyalty in the family embraces love and appreciation and is evidenced by a willingness to sacrifice for and serve one another.

Loyalty to Friends

Loyalty to friends makes it possible for them to rely on us and us on them. What a wonderful sense of security this brings!

Loyalty to Employer

In our business relations, loyalty to our employer is most vital. This means being faithful and trustworthy and giving to the best of our ability, recognizing that our employer's success is reflected in our welfare. Loyalty produces power and effectiveness. An ounce of loyalty is worth a pound of cleverness.

Loyalty to Country

It is traditional that those elected or appointed to governmental positions take an oath of allegiance. Public servants must be loyal to the office to which they are elected or appointed. Disloyalty brings distrust and can result in impeachment or dismissal.

We know that the Constitution of the United States is a divinely established document, and that it "should be maintained for the rights and protection of all flesh, according to just and holy principles." (D&C 101:77.)

The position of the Church in this matter is clearly stated in the twelfth Article of Faith: "We believe in being subject to kings, presidents, rulers, and magistrates, in obeying, honoring, and sustaining the law."

Loyalty to Church and God

An interesting experience is told of Elder J. Golden Kimball. In speaking to a meeting of Saints on the subject of tithing he said, "All of you who would be willing to die for the gospel please put up your hands." Nearly every hand in the congregation was raised. Then he said, "All of you who have been paying an honest tithing please raise your hands." Only a few hands were raised. Elder Kimball then turned to the bishop and said, "See, they would rather die than pay their tithing."

Tithing, of course, is only one of God's commandments that tests our loyalty. Loyalty to God and church, simply stated, means doing God's will without reservations. Our Lord and Savior set the pattern of loyalty in Gethsemane when in his prayer to the Father He said, "Father, all things are possible unto thee; take away this cup from me: nevertheless not what I will, but what thou wilt." (Mark 14:36.)

Judas set the pattern for disloyalty as he betrayed his master, the Christ. He later became remorseful, but under the influence of Satan, he hanged himself, the final chapter of his disloyalty.

The great dedication of the Prophet Joseph Smith and other mighty men of modern Israel illustrates the meaning of loyalty to God and to church. The Lord has told us: "Let no man be afraid to lay down his life for my sake; for whoso layeth down his life for my sake shall find it again. And whoso is not willing to lay down his life for my sake is not my disciple." (D&C 103:27-28.)

Loyalty Is Our Choice

In considering things as they are, in considering the need for honesty and consistency in living, and in considering the need for greater freedom, let us never forget that we must choose where we place our loyalties. As Joshua of old declared, "Choose you this day whom ye will serve; . . . as for me and my house, we will serve the Lord." (Josh. 24:15.)

There are many today who have chosen to serve the Lord and are giving much, yes, even their lives, for true freedom principles that bring real happiness, growth, and development. On the other hand, there are others who are loyal to false freedom principles that would, if they prevailed, destroy us as individuals and as a country. We must always remember that what we do, far more than what we say, shows where our loyalties are.

Live for True Freedom

May we live for true freedom, choose the right, do what we ought to do, and make the choice that Joshua did—to serve the Lord. We must never give our loyalty to a cause that will bring a false freedom of delusion, counterfeit happiness, failure, and eventual destruction. Our loyalties set the pattern for our lives and eventually become a way of life for us.

Loyalty to self, to family, to friends, to employers, to country, and to church and God will assure us true freedom and independence and result in peace, achievement, happiness, and eventually eternal life. Let us all, as in the words of our glorious hymn, commit ourselves to be—

> True to the faith that our parents have cherished,
> True to the truth for which martyrs have perished,
> To God's command,
> Soul, heart, and hand,
> Faithful and true we will ever stand.
>
> —Hymns, no. 157

Missionaries and Missionary Work

The Savior's Charge

Jesus told His disciples in the meridian of time that they should "go . . . and teach all nations, baptizing them in the name of the Father, and of the Son, and of the Holy Ghost: teaching them to observe all things whatsoever I have commanded you." (Matt. 28:19-20.)

The Savior has given us this same charge in this dispensation through the Prophet Joseph Smith and the prophets who have followed him.

Missions Change Missionaries' Lives

Not only does the gospel change the lives of those whom the missionaries teach and bring into the Church, but also the lives of the missionaries themselves are changed. As instruments in the hands of the Lord, they, by bringing souls into the kingdom of God, receive not only joy, happiness, peace, and contentment, but also growth and development.

Our missionaries have accepted today's challenge. They are developing important leadership abilities that will be of value to them in their homes and in their business, Church, and social lives. This will be the same with you as you fulfill an honorable mission.

There are many ways to develop the missionary spirit and a genuine desire to go on a mission. Be well prepared for the great challenges that lie ahead in the mission field. As you prepare yourself, you will be increasing your capacity to motivate, stimulate, encourage, strengthen, and inspire others.

Develop the Desire to Serve a Mission

Each of us must make many decisions during a lifetime that can greatly affect our happiness, our growth, and our development. My experiences as a young missionary have been most helpful to me in my home, business, Church, and government activities.

You should not go on a mission just because your parents want you to go, or because all of your buddies have gone; you should go only when you have a genuine desire. But set as your goal the development of such a desire and the preparing of yourself.

The Dream of a Mission

A line from the musical *South Pacific* says, "You gotta have a dream." Then the song explains, "If you don't have a dream, how you gonna have a dream come true?" What are your dreams? What do you aspire to?

When I was a young man, one of the things I aspired to was a mission, a dream that I think is a worthy goal for any young man or woman in the Church. At that time, missions weren't emphasized in the same way as they are today, but I am certain my family was an important factor in my decision.

I remember hearing my grandmother, Jane Snyder Richards, tell me stories about my grandfather. I had been named for him, and though he died before I was born, I admired him very much. He had been a fine missionary and had gone on several missions during his lifetime. I'm sure that influenced me.

Another factor was my older brother—I was the youngest of six. He was serving in the Eastern States Mission when his mission president died, and he was asked to act as mission president until a replacement could be found. His diligence and testimony greatly impressed me as a young man.

So I think my heritage in the Church influenced me deeply as I made my decision, but it was not the only factor. I had already begun my college education when I was interviewed by the bishop about going on a mission. In addition, I had previously received a flattering and tempting offer—an appointment to the U.S. Naval Academy at Annapolis, Maryland, where I knew that I would receive one of the finest educations available at that time. I remember sitting down in my room and thinking, "Well, Frank, where do you want to go? Where will Annapolis take you? And where will a mission take you?"

Fifty-five years later, and with a testimony much strengthened by a lifetime of experiences gained by serving the Lord, I know that I made the right decision in going on a mission, and I have been grateful to my Heavenly Father that I had enough faith in Him and enough love for the Church that I was willing to make that decision.

I recall that as my children were growing up, I frequently told them about my earlier missionary experiences and counseled them to prepare for a mission. I told them I hoped they would be able to have both a mission and a college education; but if it ever came to a question of being able to have only one, I would recommend a mission as being much more important and helpful than a college education. Fortunately, they were each able to have both a mission and a college education.

My wife and I have felt deep joy and pride in our children as they've grown up and we've seen them make right decisions. Our two sons and one of our daughters went on missions. We've still got the letters that they wrote on their missions, radiating joy and happiness at their blessings from being able to serve the Lord in that way. Our youngest son was later called to preside over a mission, and we felt happiness and gratitude for the wonderful experiences he and his wife had.

Ten Reasons for a Mission

Without question the greatest challenge and opportunity to develop leadership afforded young members of the Church is missionary work. I can hear some say, "Specifically, *why* should I go on a mission?" There are many really good reasons why you should go on a mission, or even several missions, in your lifetime. Ten that quickly come to my mind are:

1. Because it will offer you the most superb way of serving your fellowmen—through giving them the opportunity to learn of the restored gospel of Jesus Christ and to become members of His Church, a gift of eternal value.

2. Because you have been charged by your Father in heaven with the responsibility of taking the gospel message to His children.

3. Because it is not an easy assignment, and one grows only by hard work and learning how to solve difficult problems. Charles F. Kettering, one-time president of General Motors Corporation, frequently said to his associates, "Problems are the price of progress. Don't bring me anything but trouble. Good news weakens me. Bring me problems, because they strengthen me." What a wonderful philosophy! Problems viewed in this way are opportunities to make men and women strong. Performing honorable missions likewise makes men and women strong.

4. Because it will prepare you to succeed in every area of life. You will develop faith in the Lord Jesus Christ and yourself.

5. Because it will be the happiest and most profitable period in your life up to that time.

6. Because it will present opportunities to travel and develop culturally and spiritually.

7. Because it is the best way to build your testimony.

8. Because it presents constant opportunities to learn how to get along with people.

9. Because it develops the habit of study and increases one's appetite for knowledge.

10. Because every day in every way it develops leadership abilities.

These reasons and promises are based on your magnifying your calling when and if you are called on a mission.

Women Make Good Missionaries

President Kimball was inspired when he asked every worthy young man to go on a mission and every young woman to live so as to be worthy to go on a mission. Of course, young women are not encouraged to go on missions in the same way that young men are. If a young woman is in love with a worthy man, we don't feel that their relationship should be interrupted by a mission call to her. However, many young women are not in that situation; and if one desires and is worthy to go on a mission, she could be called.

My experience has indicated that sister missionaries are as effective as elders in leading people to baptism, and that a mission gives a woman as much benefit in her later life as it does an elder. She becomes a better wife, a better mother, a better Relief Society president, better at her career—just better in every way.

So a mission is a worthy goal for every young Latter-day Saint.

Spirituality, the First Requirement

Mere human reason is insufficient to lead men to a testimony of the gospel of Jesus Christ, for "the things of God

knoweth no man, but [by] the Spirit of God." (1 Cor. 2:11.)
Thus, spirituality is required for missionary service.

Speaking to the elders, priests, and teachers through the
Prophet Joseph Smith, the Lord said: "And the Spirit shall be
given unto you by the prayer of faith; and if ye receive not the
Spirit ye shall not teach." (D&C 42:14.)

President Brigham Young said, "I would rather hear an
Elder, either here or in the world, speak only five words accompanied by the power of God, and they would do more good than
to hear long sermons without the Spirit." (*Discourses of Brigham
Young*, p. 330.)

Another condition of spirituality is that we love one
another. The Savior was the greatest missionary because of his
surpassing love. You can't teach the gospel to a man you don't
love. Love is the distinguishing mark of true followers of
Christ. Only as we lose our lives in the service of others can we
truly find them.

Faith Is Necessary

"All things are possible," said the Savior, "to him that believeth." (Mark 9:23.)

To make the most of every contact with a nonmember of
the Church, approach him with the confidence that you have
not been called of God to fail, but to succeed. Above all, remember that faith is the gift of God to those who live worthy of
it by doing all that is in their own power, relying on God for the
rest. This is the heart of the preparation of a missionary.

Sometimes we don't receive the blessings that we might receive because there is fear in our hearts, and we don't do the
things that merit the blessing. But the Lord has promised, "If ye
are prepared ye shall not fear." (D&C 38:30.)

President David O. McKay called the General Authorities
into the temple on one occasion a few years ago. We went in
fasting and with prayers in our hearts, partook of the sacra-

ment, and spent much of the day in soul-searching. President McKay talked to us about the matter of fear. He said, "Do not be afraid. Nothing will hurt you as you keep the Lord's commandments." The Lord has said, "I, the Lord, am bound when ye do what I say; but when ye do not what I say, ye have no promise." (D&C 82:10.)

Study Two Hours a Day

In connection with preparation of the missionary, one thing is very vital, and that is study. Don't overlook your study periods. I would recommend that you study at least two hours a day, one hour on discussions and the other hour on your personal studies. As far as I am concerned, I limit my study pretty much to the four standard works of the Church. You don't have enough time to study a lot of other things in the mission field. I suggest that you study the four standard works of the Church.

Thoughtful, prayerful study of the scriptures is an essential source of faith and inspiration to the missionary. Elder Thomas S. Monson has said, "The scriptures testify of God and contain the words of eternal life. They become the burden of your message—even the tools of your trade. Your confidence will be directly related to your knowledge of God's word." (*Conference Report*, October 4, 1969, p. 93.)

High Baptism Standards

Our missionary program is based on declaring repentance and baptism. Our missionaries know that baptism is essential, and they are baptism–conscious. In section 20 of the Doctrine and Covenants the Lord has given us a list of qualifications necessary for baptism. Missionaries are instructed to see that these qualifications are met. This is not a day for compromising standards.

In the Doctrine and Covenants, the Lord says, "Wherefore,

I give unto you a commandment that ye go among this people, and say unto them, like unto mine apostle of old, whose name was Peter: Believe on the name of the Lord Jesus, who was on the earth, and is to come, the beginning and the end; repent and be baptized in the name of Jesus Christ, according to the holy commandment, for the remission of sins." (D&C 49: 11-13.)

After baptism, our responsibility is to fellowship the new converts. There will be little falling away as we love these good people into the Church and give them an opportunity to serve.

Instruments for the Holy Ghost

The missionary discussions are not designed to convince intellectually, but rather, they are instruments through which the Holy Ghost can work to awaken a spiritual awareness and bring a personal testimony into the hearts of the listeners that Joseph Smith is a prophet and that the Church is true.

Many contacts, after participating in the discussions and listening to the testimonies of the missionaries, ask, "How may I obtain this knowledge and receive a testimony?" A prophet of the Lord has said that if an earnest seeker of truth will ask God with a sincere heart, with real intent, having faith in Christ, he will have manifested to him, by the Holy Ghost, a testimony that these things are true. (See Moro. 10:4–5.)

Some members fear that their friends may be offended by these discussions. However, most nonmembers are pleased by the opportunity given in the dialogues to learn basic Mormon doctrine and to draw their own conclusions. An example is the question asked in the first discussion about baptism. After a discussion of the restoration of the priesthood, the missionary asks: "As you come to know in your own heart that this is true, will you be baptized by someone having the priesthood?" The experience of missionaries is that most people are not offended by this question; rather, they often indicate they will be baptized if they come to know the Church is true.

Obey Mission Rules

I have seen so many incidents happen to missionaries that have brought trouble and remorse into their lives as a result of their not following the rules that have been given for their protection, for the upbuilding of the kingdom, and for the protection of the Church. One of the very first rules that I always mention as I interview missionaries and talk to them is the responsibility of keeping themselves clean and unspotted from the sins of the world. Never leave your companion. That's one of the first rules that's given to you. And as you stay with your companion, you're not subject to temptations that might come into your life were you to violate that requirement or rule.

Make Yours a Success Story

When I was released as a mission president, the mission president who succeeded me asked every missionary to write a letter to Sister Richards and me. Of course, we didn't know anything about it until we received the letters. I would say that ninety percent of the missionaries said somewhere in their letters that one thing above all else that they loved us for was because we instilled within them the attitude of success.

My prayer is that every missionary in the Church might gain this same attitude as he serves the Lord. Great blessings will come to those who serve Him with all their might, mind, and strength.

Missionary Efforts by Members

Our Charge

The Savior has told us that "this is a day of warning, and not a day of many words." (D&C 63:58.) Thus, Peter's sermon on the Day of Pentecost was Christ. His hearers were "pricked" in their hearts and said to Peter and the rest of the apostles, "Men and brethren, what shall we do?" Peter told them, "Repent, and be baptized every one of you in the name of Jesus Christ." (Acts 2:37-38.)

Through the Prophet Joseph Smith, the Savior has given us this charge: "Go among this people, and say unto them, like unto mine apostle of old, whose name was Peter: Believe on the name of the Lord Jesus, . . . Repent and be baptized." (D&C 49:11-13.)

The Lord has also said: "If it so be that you should labor all your days in crying repentance unto this people, and bring, save it be one soul unto me, how great shall be your joy in the kingdom of my Father! And now, if your joy will be great with one soul that you have brought unto me into the kingdom of my Father, how great will be your joy if you should bring many souls unto me!" (D&C 18:15-16.)

Finding the Elect

In the Doctrine and Covenants, the Lord tells us, "Ye are called to bring to pass the gathering of mine elect; for mine elect hear my voice and harden not their hearts." (D&C 29:7.)

I am sure that there are many elect in all parts of the world. It is our responsibility to find interested people for the missionaries to teach, and to fellowship these people before and after baptism.

Members of the Church may regret their inability to do missionary work abroad while ignoring the opportunities at home. President George Albert Smith said: "It is not necessary for you to be called to go into the mission field in order to proclaim the truth. Begin on the man who lives next door by inspiring confidence in him, by inspiring love in him for you because of your righteousness, and your missionary work has already begun." (*Conference Report,* Oct. 7, 1961, p. 51.)

In the words of President David O. McKay: "We are all missionaries. We may drop a word here, bear our testimony, be an exemplar by what we do; and, as we accept this call and discharge our duties in the stakes, wards, quorums, and the mission field, our acts will 'roll from soul to soul and go forever and forever.'" (*Conference Report,* Oct. 4, 1969, p. 87.)

The Potential for Missionary Work

I am continually amazed and pleased as I travel throughout the missions and the stakes of the Church to find so many members accepting the admonition to be missionaries. How many of you have had the joy of seeing your friends and neighbors take an interest in the Church and be baptized because of your being a member missionary?

One of the important characteristics of the Church of Jesus Christ is missionary activity. The Savior has charged us to "teach all nations, baptizing them in the name of the Father, and of the Son, and of the Holy Ghost." (Matt. 28:19.) And "every nation" includes our friends and the people we casually meet, regardless of where we live.

The question is: How can we, a relatively small group, accomplish this great responsibility? Certainly not with the number of full-time stake and district missionaries we now have, regardless of how good they are!

Less Time Finding—More Time Teaching

In the past, missionaries generally spent most of their time finding interested persons to teach and a small part of their time in teaching. Now the "every member a missionary" plan gives the members a chance to do missionary work by finding interested persons for the missionaries to teach. This greatly increases the effectiveness of the missionaries. They can teach many more people, particularly as they are taught in groups.

In working with the missions on the East Coast, I have found that the great increase in convert baptisms, and especially baptisms of entire families, is more and more attributable to the fact that a greater number of members are finding interested persons for the missionaries to teach, and the members are loving it.

We had the opportunity to meet many of these wonderful members and hear their exciting and happy experiences. I am confident that there are thousands of members of the Church who have a sincere desire to do missionary work but don't know how to do it or what to do. How, then, can a member, regardless of age or sex, become an effective missionary within the meaning of the prophet's admonition, "Every member a missionary"?

Three Ways to Find Contacts

You ask, what can I do? Well, you can find persons who would like to know more about the Church. But how can you find such persons? The following three ways are pretty much the basis of the "every member a missionary" program.

First, live the gospel. As your friends and neighbors feel your love, they will want to know more about the Church.

Second, ask people what they know about the Church and if they would like to know more. Yes, ask the golden questions.

Third, take your friends and neighbors to Church meetings and socials.

All three ways are part of the referral program as you arrange for the missionaries to teach the interested persons. When you find interested persons—by personal contact, over the telephone, or by correspondence—bring them into your home, preferably in a group, and ask the missionaries in to give them the discussions. If they are out of the area, send their names to the Missionary Department of the Church in Salt Lake City, together with details of how you secured the name and other pertinent information, and the referral will be sent to the proper mission.

Let me elaborate on the three ways you can find persons who want to know more about the Church by giving you a few examples.

Go the Second Mile

The first way to find interested persons is to live the gospel.

Some time ago I was showing a couple around Temple Square. They were very interested, particularly when Brother Alexander Schreiner, who was then the Tabernacle organist, took an active interest in them, showing them the organ and how it is played. Brother Schreiner really went the extra mile. I asked the couple if they knew any members of the Church in Iowa. They replied, "Yes, a wonderful family." Recently, when a friend of theirs had a baby, this Mormon family took the children of the woman who was having the baby into their home while the mother was in the hospital. Both Brother Schreiner and the Iowa family were evidencing their love for their fellowmen. These incidents have been an important factor in interesting this couple. They expressed a desire to know more about the Church.

"Let your light so shine before men, that they may see your good works, and glorify your Father which is in heaven." (Matt. 5:16.) President Harold B. Lee, in touring the Northwestern States Mission, said: "This means to let your light so shine that men shall be led to join the Church, or the kingdom of God."

Ask the Golden Questions

The second way to be a member missionary is to ask the golden questions as you meet people personally, or over the telephone, or through the mail. I have asked the golden questions hundreds of times, and I have never embarrassed myself or the person I asked. Once, when I was registering in a motel in Raleigh, North Carolina, I asked the golden questions of the young man at the desk. He was not interested, but the man standing behind him overheard our conversation. He had been to Salt Lake City, was impressed, and wanted to know more. I told him we had missionaries in Raleigh, and he gave me his name and address. He was very interested in having the missionaries call and tell him more about the Church. I immediately turned this golden contact over to the missionaries.

Some time ago, while having dinner in a New York restaurant, we asked our waiter, a very fine man, the golden questions. He replied enthusiastically that he had been to Utah and California and had met several Latter-day Saint families. He was very much impressed with their way of life and wanted to know more about the Church. He gave us his address in Brooklyn and seemed anxious to have the missionaries call at his home and give him and his family the discussions. We promptly gave this good referral to the mission president in New York.

A bishop's wife in Atlanta, Georgia, wanted to do missionary work but did not know how or when she could find the time and still take care of her young family. The missionaries suggested that she "telephone proselyte," asking the golden questions over the phone from her own home in the evening after the children were in bed. She told me that the missionaries showed her how and that it was thrilling and most rewarding, and not embarrassing. She found many interested persons for the missionaries to teach.

Take Your Friends to Church

The third way to find interested persons is to take your friends and neighbors to Church meetings and socials. In Bowling Green, Kentucky, the Relief Society needed an organist. The president asked a nonmember friend to help them out. She replied that she would be glad to, and before long she became interested and was taught the gospel by the missionaries and was baptized.

In the Southern States Mission, a young girl was walking home with a friend and began humming "Come, Come, Ye Saints." Her friend said, "My, that's a beautiful melody. What is it?" The girl told her about it and made a date to take her to a Church service. After attending a few times, the friend arranged for the missionaries to teach her family. The family have all been baptized and are happy doing their part in building the kingdom.

Have You Asked Them?

I can hear some people say, "I know my friends and relatives wouldn't be interested. I've tried for years to talk to members of my family about religion, and it seems to irritate them," and other such things. But I ask, do you really know that your friends would not be interested? Have you asked them? I suggest that you do ask them.

In asking members all over the country to ask these question, many times I have sensed a feeling of skepticism. But almost always afterwards, someone has written me or sent word to me saying that although he was doubtful at first, he tried asking the questions and was happily surprised to find many responding, "Yes, I would like to know more."

Keep in mind also that young people as well as old can ask these questions, and the younger ones do not seem as hesitant as some of us older ones.

Use the Auxiliaries

Invite your friends to attend meetings of the auxiliaries with you. This is one of the easier ways that we have of sharing the gospel. You and the members of your family should not only invite these people, but also make appointments to pick them up to take them to Sunday School, Relief Society, Mutual, Primary, sacrament meeting, or any other of the Church meetings.

Likewise, you can take these people to the social functions of the auxiliary organizations. These are often very pleasant occasions for nonmembers, and when they come to feel the warmth and friendship that they find in this association, they are much more receptive to the teachings of the gospel.

A striking example happened in the Northwest. Sister Freeman, a convert of about two years, was serving as president of the Relief Society in one of the branches. There had been no missionaries in this branch for some time. We discussed the "share the gospel" plan with the members of the branch and sent two missionaries in with instructions to use the plan. Soon after they arrived, they got in touch with Sister Freeman. She later wrote to me, saying: "A special thanks for sending these fine missionaries to our branch. We are thrilled and very thankful, and we are reorganizing our visiting teaching so that the presidency will be free to visit any contacts that the missionaries ask us to."

About six months later, I was interviewing one of the elders in that area. I asked him how things were going in the branch. He said, "Simply great! Do you know how many nonmember women were out to the opening Relief Society meeting in the branch?" I guessed six or eight, which I thought would be pretty good. He said, "Thirty-four!" This is the "share the gospel" plan in action in the Relief Society. Thanks to Sister Freeman and her fine members, because of this activity many wonderful members are now enjoying the benefits of the gospel.

Members Can Hold Group Meetings

The work of missionaries in teaching the doctrine is made much easier when the members are involved in teaching processes. Members can set up cottage meetings, participate in investigator firesides, bear testimony, provide social involvement, and encourage Church activity.

One of the greatest missionary meetings recorded in scripture is described in the second chapter of the book of Acts. Peter taught a multitude consisting of "Jews, devout men, out of every nation under heaven." Preaching by the power of the Spirit, he taught them the simple truths of the first principles. "Then they that gladly received his word were baptized: and the same day there were added unto them about three thousand souls." (Acts 2:5,41.)

It is clear that the Spirit can influence groups of people. Parley P. Pratt, Wilford Woodruff, and Heber C. Kimball taught large groups of people and, as a result, converted whole families and communities. Elder Pratt reported that when he went as a missionary to Toronto, he took a letter of introduction to John Taylor, who asked a Mrs. Walton to provide lodging for Elder Pratt. Mrs. Walton responded: "Tell him I will send my son

John over to pilot him to my house, while I go and gather my relatives and friends to come in this very evening and hear him talk; for I feel by the Spirit that he is a man sent by the Lord with a message which will do us good." (*Autobiography of Parley P. Pratt* [Deseret Book, 1938], p. 136.)

That evening, a number of people gathered at Mrs. Walton's home and listened with interest to Elder Pratt. As a result of this and subsequent group meetings in Toronto, Elder Pratt baptized a number of people, including John Taylor, who later became president of the Church.

Investigators' Firesides

An investigator fireside is, in effect, a testimony meeting for nonmembers. In an informal environment, a group of nonmembers are invited to introduce themselves and tell what it is they like about the Church. Many of them will bear strong testimonies. The rest will be moved by what they say. This is followed by a short talk on a simple subject that may be given by a recent convert, a bishop, a Relief Society president, or some such person. After a closing prayer and song, light refreshments are served, and those present have an opportunity for social mingling.

Members of the Church can cooperate by opening their homes for investigator firesides, providing refreshments, accepting assignments to speak, and being skillful hosts. Wherever possible, however, the investigators should assume some responsibility for the arrangements.

Military Missionaries

Another area that must not be overlooked is our men and women serving in the military. These men and women can be and many are real missionaries. As they live their religion, they are respected and admired by their associates. They can be instrumental in bringing untold numbers of converts into the Church and developing thousands of referrals each year for the missionaries.

The Vital Role of Fellowshipping

Fellowshipping is a vital part of the conversion process. Fellowshipping frequently becomes a part of the finding process. As I recall, Elder Mark E. Petersen once said, "Conversion without fellowshipping is as ineffective as baptism without confirmation."

Several revelations were given to the Prophet Joseph Smith relative to the members participating in missionary work. In the eleventh section of the Doctrine and Covenants, verses 3 and 4, we are told, "Behold, the field is white already to harvest; therefore, whoso desireth to reap let him thrust in his sickle with his might, and reap while the day lasts, that he may treasure up for his soul everlasting salvation in the kingdom of God. Yea, whosoever will thrust in his sickle and reap, the same is called of God."

Nonmembers who are reluctant to meet with missionaries are often willing and eager to participate in activities sponsored by the Church and to mingle socially with the members of the Church. In these circumstances, it becomes possible to teach them the gospel by example. They are much more likely to respond favorably to an invitation to be taught the doctrine.

Help Nonmembers Attend Church Comfortably

Nonmembers receiving the missionary discussions should be attending sacrament meeting and Sunday School on a regular basis. Invite them to attend with you and follow up by arranging transportation, if necessary or desirable.

Many nonmembers who are attracted by their LDS friends and who respond favorably to the missionary discussions are nevertheless reluctant to attend our church services. In part, they fear the possible embarrassment of not being familiar with the service. To help remove the fear of unfamiliar procedures, take time to explain to them beforehand what to expect.

They may also fear the awkward sensation of being obvious newcomers and strangers. Nonmembers will feel less like strangers when they know members of the ward or branch before they attend church. The very fact that you take them to Church solves much of the problem. You may also help by introducing them to the bishop or branch president, auxiliary heads, and other investigators or recent converts.

Are Converts Staying in the Church?

Many ask if the converts staying in the Church are remaining active. Yes, where fellowshipping is effective, generally a high percentage of the converts remain active. Fellowshipping, however, includes loving converts into the Church and giving them work assignments. It is not unusual to hear converts say, "It's a great feeling to be needed."

It is recommended that each new convert be given a position in the Church; many would make excellent stake missionaries. These new members are like the saints of old to whom the Apostle Paul wrote: "Ye are no more strangers and foreigners, but fellowcitizens with the saints, and of the household of God." (Eph. 2:19.)

The Dryland Mormon

Some time ago, I was in Georgia to dedicate a chapel. As I was walking around in the chapel prior to its dedication, a man came up to me and introduced himself. "I'm a dryland Mormon," he said. I replied, "What do you mean, a dryland Mormon?" He said, "Well, my wife and family are members of the Church, and I come to church quite frequently. I don't smoke or drink, and I have made contributions to the Church, but I've never been baptized." I took him by the lapels, looked him in the eye, and told him there was no such thing as a dryland Mormon.

I said that when Nicodemus came to Christ and asked him what he should do, Christ told him he had to be born again. When Nicodemus could not understand that, the Savior said, "Verily, verily, I say unto thee, Except a man be born of the water and of the Spirit, he cannot enter into the kingdom of God." (John 3:5.)

"And so," I said to this man, "you are denying yourself and your family great blessings by not being baptized. The blessings that await you are, first, a remission of your sins, and second, the receipt of the Holy Ghost."

I continued, "When you have been baptized by water and then have hands laid on your head to receive the Holy Ghost, you will receive a power that will guide and direct your life and will open up the way to greater blessings, such as receiving the priesthood and an opportunity to go into the house of the Lord to receive sealing ordinances that will make your wife and family yours throughout eternity. Now all of these things are dependent upon your being baptized. I would recommend to you that you ask the branch president to interview you to see if you are worthy to be baptized, and if you are worthy, I would recommend that you set your baptism date right away."

After the dedicatory service, people were coming up to talk with me, and this man and his wife came up. Both were in tears as the man shook hands with me and said, "President Richards, I want to be interviewed for baptism." He was interviewed that night by the branch president, was found worthy, and was baptized.

Sharing Increases Spirituality

Yes, baptism is necessary, and we must be baptism-conscious. On several occasions, bishops and branch presidents have said to me, "President, having all of these people coming into the Church is wonderful. We need them." Where members are sharing the gospel with friends, many very fine converts are coming into the Church, many of whom make wonderful leaders almost immediately after baptism.

In addition, great blessings are received by members who participate in the "share the gospel" plan. Many who had been relatively inactive became active again. Increased spirituality is definitely noticeable among the ward members who are sharing. It is like love—as you give it to others, it increases in yourself.

I know this is true. Let every one of us be a missionary. It is wonderful. May we have the faith and the determination and courage to make this plan an effective vehicle in bringing great numbers of souls into the kingdom of God. Let us always keep in mind that the purpose of missionary work is to bring souls into the kingdom of God through the ordinance of baptism.

Testimony from Virginia

Soon after the "every member a missionary" program was introduced, I received a letter from the members and missionaries of the Elkins Branch in West Virginia, which indicated what was happening [in 1961]. Let me quote a part of it:

"We are so thrilled, as missionaries and members of the Elkins Branch, with the success and growth of our branch that we want to write and tell you about it. We have been blessed with this growth since you came and told us the 'every member a missionary' program. We, as a team in the Elkins Branch, began asking people the golden questions, and those who wanted to know about the Church were invited into our homes for group meetings. Because of this, the Lord blessed our branch membership with 121 convert baptisms in one year, which nearly doubled our branch membership.

"The branch president and his family have been having

group meetings in their home regularly for all age groups. Because this family has screened the people through asking the golden questions before they invite them into their home, the missionaries have baptized about twenty people from this one family's meetings alone. The effect it has had is tremendous. The people are really baptism-conscious and are doing everything they can to have group meetings.

"We testify to you that asking the golden questions and having group meetings is a very effective way to bring souls into the kingdom of God. The love, enthusiasm, and spirituality have never been higher. We love to baptize people."

Sharing a Camper

A father and his two sons from California went to Southern Utah on a fishing trip and pitched their tent in a campground between the campers of two Mormon families. It began to rain, and the Californians' tent began to leak. The Mormon families shared the warmth and hospitality of their campers with those nonmembers for several days. Even before a referral had been forwarded by the members, their guests had returned home and asked to meet with the missionaries, and shortly thereafter, the family was baptized. Such opportunities for teaching the gospel by example are given to each of us continually.

Taxicab Encounter

While on a business trip to Calgary, Canada, a member of the Church from Utah was asked by a taxi driver if he was a Mormon. Although he had always felt hesitant before, he took this opportunity to ask the golden questions. He was surprised at the driver's interest in learning more. He sent referrals to the mission president, and within a few short weeks, the taxi driver and his family had joined the Church.

The use of the golden questions has proven to be highly successful without embarrassing either the member or the non-member. The opportunity to ask the golden questions should not be limited to nonmembers living within the boundaries of a particular ward or stake. The missionary-minded member will find opportunities to ask visitors in his own area, business acquaintances, friends, and relatives who live in other areas, and those he meets in his own travels.

She Is Mine

At a stake conference in California, great interest was shown in the "every member a missionary" program. After the Sunday morning session, a woman came up and introduced herself and presented her friend, saying, "She is mine." Both of their faces reflected great joy and happiness. Then she explained that she had asked her friend the golden questions, and her friend had replied that she was interested and would like to know more about the Church. The woman arranged for the missionaries to come to her home and teach her friend the beautiful truths of the gospel as contained in the missionary discussions. Her friend prayed, studied, and attended church to further her understanding. She soon gained a testimony and was baptized. No wonder this good sister felt so much joy as she put her arm around her friend and said, "She is mine."

Influence of the Tabernacle Choir

We were in Canada some time ago, and as we were going into Toronto, we were sitting by a man who was the eastern representative of the Curtis Publishing Company. I told him we were Mormon missionaries from Salt Lake City and asked, "What do you know about the Mormon Church?" He said, "Why, my wife and my family listen to the Tabernacle Choir every Sunday morning." He added, "It's wonderful. I have bought every record that the Tabernacle Choir has put out." I said, "Would you like to know more about the Mormon Church?" He said, "I would like to know more about the Mormon Church because of the beautiful music it produces." And so we turned that referral over to the missionaries.

Long Beach, California

While attending a stake conference in Long Beach, California, I was told that one of the wards had a project of gathering newspapers. A young boy, while collecting papers from the neighbors, asked the golden questions. Two families said they would like to know more about the Church, and they were subsequently taught and baptized by the missionaries.

Charlottesville, Virginia

In Charlottesville, Virginia, one of our good sisters who worked at a bakery decided to ask the five women with whom she was working the golden questions. All of them said they would like to know more about the Church. She invited them to a series of group meetings in her home to hear the missionaries, and four of the five women gained testimonies and were baptized into the Church.

One of the most powerful forces in the Church is and always has been its youth. They love their friends and are not afraid to ask them the golden questions. After a young boy from Charlottesville, Virginia, was baptized, he went home and said to his grandmother, "Grandma, you haven't been baptized into the true church." She said, "Maybe I haven't. Who told you this?" He told her the Mormon elders did. She said, "Send them to me." He did, and the grandmother was taught the gospel and was baptized.

Atlanta, Georgia

Sister Kemp of Atlanta, Georgia, told how she had earnestly prayed that the Lord would bless her with wisdom and understanding in raising her thirteen-year-old daughter and her two sons, who were sixteen and fourteen. Shortly after she prayed, her sons brought two Mormon elders home. Sister Kemp knew that her prayers had been answered. After the missionaries gave the family the discussions, the children asked for baptism, but the parents were not ready. As the Kemps witnessed the baptisms, their daughter came out of the water and threw her wet arms around her mother, saying, "Mommy, I know this is the Church of Jesus Christ." Shortly after, her parents requested baptism. Surely the Lord moves in a mysterious way, his wonders to perform.

Two Personal Experiences

As I was flying to Chicago some time ago, I sat by a young college student from Des Moines, Iowa, who had been attending Utah State University. He stated that he had made many friends who were Mormons and had been given a copy of the Book of Mormon. I asked, "Would you like to know more about the Mormon Church?" He liked the idea. He gave me his name and address, and I told him I would arrange to have two missionaries come by to see him. I sent the referral to the mission president in Des Moines, and a few weeks later I received word from the missionaries that they had baptized the student and were teaching his parents and his brothers and sisters.

On another occasion, I was privileged to baptize a man whose wife and family had been members for many years. He had been taught the gospel by missionaries and really understood the doctrines. When I challenged him to be baptized, she accepted. Afterwards he told me that I was the first person to challenge him to be baptized.

Testimony of Missionary Work

The thing that keeps Sister Richards and me personally excited about doing missionary work is the joy of doing it successfully, the joy it brings to others.

I am grateful that the Lord has let the prophets know that we are to be involved in missionary work all our lives. I have seen how our lives can be enriched by becoming the link between nonmembers and missionaries, by helping others to mold themselves into a new life-style and circle of friends, and by helping them find the answer to their question, "What is the purpose of life?"

We are engaged in building the kingdom of God. As President Spencer W. Kimball has asked us to "lengthen our stride" in missionary work, may I suggest that we all do this by increasing our effectiveness in finding and friendshipping the elect. I sincerely pray that the choice blessings of our Father in heaven will be with each of us as we do this.

Motherhood

Honor Thy Mother

When the Lord called Moses up to the top of Mount Sinai and gave him the Ten Commandments, the first commandment with a promise was: "Honour thy father and thy mother." The promise for obedience was: "That thy days may be long upon the land which the Lord thy God giveth thee." (Ex. 20:12.) No love in all the world can equal the love of a true mother. Her love is life, strength, and encouragement. In her every act, she teaches us that the true values of life are the simple things and that honest living really pays.

Motherhood Is Synonymous with Service

Motherhood is another name for service and sacrifice. From birth a mother hourly and daily gives of her life to her loved ones. For her consecrated devotion she asks nothing in return. If her love is reciprocated, she is content; if not, she still loves on. She asks nothing for the roses she transplants from her own cheeks to those of her loved ones, nothing for the hours of vigilance during days and nights of sickness, nothing for the thousand self-denials and sacrifices that have to be made that the children might receive proper schooling, nothing for the heartaches caused by a thoughtless word or act.

For all this and a thousand other things incident to motherhood, mother asks nothing but deserves much. For kindness, she deserves kindness; for tenderness, she should be given tenderness; for self-sacrifice, she merits a little self-denial on the part of the children; for love, she should be given love.

By her example she is daily teaching us the real virtues of life—how to love and work, to worship and repent, to have faith and self-respect, to be honest and courageous, to serve and be devoted, to be charitable and just.

A Mother's Lessons

In teaching us these virtues and many others, mother teaches us that love and understanding at home depend upon the ability of every member of the family to work, grow, and pray together; that material prosperity is not the test of mental, moral, or spiritual growth; that the spiritual is the divine in man. In preparing our daily food, she teaches us that it is only of value if it is transformed into blood, brawn, nerve, and tissue; that spiritual food is worthless to us unless it is transformed into finer thoughts, better acts, and nobler living, for spiritual food, like the manna from heaven given to the children of Israel in the wilderness, becomes worthless unless it is used and put to service.

Our mothers look upon life as a glorious privilege of fine service rather than dull servitude, of splendid giving rather than petty getting.

It is a wonderful thing to have someone believe in you. This is one of the great benefits of mother love. Mother love idealizes its object. It exaggerates little tendencies into great virtues, possibilities, and genius. Where much is expected from an individual, he may rise and make the dream come true.

Our beloved President David O. McKay had this to say: "Motherhood is the one thing in all the world which most truly exemplifies the God-given virtues of creating and sacrificing. Though it carries the woman close to the brink of death, motherhood also leads her into the very realm of the fountains

of life and makes her a co-partner with the Creator in bestow-
ing upon eternal spirits mortal life." (*Gospel Ideals* [Salt Lake
City: Improvement Era, 1953], p. 456.)

Making Mother Happy

As Mother gave us life, we should show her our appreciation in words and deeds every day of our lives. We need no suggestions on how to make mother happy on Mother's Day as on
every day in the year. If we give her a white carnation, she will
be pleased; if we tell her in a letter of our appreciation and love,
she will shed tears of happiness; but if we keep the spotless character and purity of soul she has given us and give her assurance
thereof, she will thank God for us and rejoice as the most
blessed of mothers.

The commandment "Honour thy father and thy mother" is
eternal and is as binding and timely today as when it was given
to a prophet of God on Mount Sinai thousands of years ago.
May God grant that we may every day in every way honor our
mothers, that our days may be long and full of joy upon this
land the Lord has given us.

Obedience

Our Cause for Rejoicing

Let us be grateful that we live in an age when the gospel of Jesus Christ has been restored in its fulness. Let us rejoice that we are privileged to be members of The Church of Jesus Christ of Latter-day Saints and have a testimony that God lives and that Jesus is the Christ.

Let me share a promise I heard Joseph Fielding Smith make. He said: "I feel in my heart to bless the faithful members of the Church. Just as surely as they continue to walk in paths of truth and virtue, they shall have the desires of their hearts in righteousness."

The Power of an Ideal

In considering the purpose of life, the Prophet Joseph Smith said: "Happiness is the object and design of our existence; and will be the end thereof, if we pursue that path that leads to it; and this path is virtue, uprightness, faithfulness, holiness, and keeping all the commandments of God." (*History of the Church* 5:134-35.)

Our Lord and Savior Jesus Christ set in His life the pattern for us to follow in our quest for this eternal joy and happiness. He admonished His disciples to be perfect, "even as your Father which is in heaven is perfect." (Matt. 5:48.)

There is tremendous power in focusing upon an ideal.

People are inclined to become like those whom they admire. As we increase our knowledge and love of the Savior and indicate our willingness to do His will, we become more perfect and like Him.

"Thy Will Be Done"

Some of the Savior's greatest attributes and most profound teachings are to be found in the incidents immediately preceding His crucifixion.

After the last supper, He and the eleven apostles left the house in which they had eaten and walked to the olive grove known as Gethsemane, on the slope of Mt. Olivet. Jesus apparently frequented this grove or garden when He desired privacy for prayer. He left eight of the apostles near the entrance with the suggestion, "Sit ye here, while I go and pray yonder." (Matt. 26:36.)

Peter, James, and John accompanied Him further, and "then saith he unto them, My soul is exceeding sorrowful, even unto death: tarry ye here, and watch with me. And he went a little further, and fell on his face, and prayed, saying, O my Father, if it be possible, let this cup pass from me: nevertheless not as I will, but as thou wilt." (Matt. 26:36-39.)

The life of the Savior is replete with instances where He applied the principle of "Thy will be done—not mine." His ability to apply this principle in His life made it possible for Him to become perfect. As we apply this principle in our lives, we likewise will move toward perfection and true happiness.

Learning God's Will

How can we know God's will in order to make our life conform? The Savior said, "If ye love me, keep my commandments." (John 14:15.)

We must so live that the Holy Ghost will guide and direct

us. We must seek to grow in knowledge, wisdom, and understanding by continuous study and contemplation of the words of Christ and those whom God has appointed to teach and instruct us. And we must pray always, remembering the promise given to us: "Draw near unto me and I will draw near unto you." (D&C 88:63.)

Accepting God's Will

This doctrine or philosophy requires one to love the Lord deeply and have great faith in His judgment. Let me illustrate.

In the prayer offered by the Prophet Joseph Smith at the dedication of the Kirtland Temple, which prayer was given to him by revelation, he said, "Help thy servants to say, with thy grace assisting them: Thy will be done, O Lord, and not ours." (D&C 109:44.)

In the fall of 1834, the Prophet was busily engaged in preparing for the School of the Elders and wrote in his diary, "No month ever found me more busily engaged than November; but as my life consisted of activity and unyielding exertions, I made this my rule: *When the Lord commands, do it.*" (*History of the Church* 2:170.)

Here again is evidenced the spirit of "Thy will be done." Joseph Smith's life exemplified this great principle.

President Brigham Young's feeling about this divine principle is recorded in a letter to Orson Spencer in June 1848, when he said, "The Lord's will is my will all the time, as he dictates so I will perform." (*Messages of the First Presidency*, ed. James R. Clark [Salt Lake City: Bookcraft, 1965], 1:338.)

Some of you are converts to the Church. Did you find it difficult to accept baptism when you felt it would mean being estranged from your family or friends, losing the security of your social position, maybe even losing your job or employment? But in your heart you *knew* it was the will of God that you should accept Him and become a member of His Church—because the Holy Ghost had borne this witness to you.

When you had the will to say "Not my will but thy will be done"—placing your trust in God and, by your acceptance of baptism, showing your faith and humility—didn't you find that you had just opened the way for God to give you greater blessings than you had ever known before?

Brother and Sister Alvarez, two wonderful young people I met in Mexico, told me that after their baptism, rather than the estrangement from family and friends they had feared, they were finding new love and respect being given to them, besides all the wonderful new friends that they had found among their brothers and sisters in the Church. They had prospered materially, and, above all, they had found a peace and nearness to their Heavenly Father that they had never known before.

My Personal Tests

As a young man I was offered an appointment to the U.S. Naval Academy. This was an honor and a real temptation. However, early in my life I had definitely decided that I would like to go on a mission, and I could now see that if I accepted the Naval Academy appointment, I probably would not be able to serve as a missionary.

After prayerful consideration I declined the appointment, as I felt it was the will of the Lord that I go on a mission. Soon thereafter I received a call to serve in the Eastern States Mission.

I will be eternally grateful for the call I received, because it was in the mission field that I learned to love the gospel, learned the power of faith, and felt the happiness and peace that come when one is responsive to the whisperings of the Holy Spirit. The pattern I set in the mission field has been a guide to me throughout my life.

My mission president, Brigham H. Roberts, in his letter of

release to me, promised me that I would "find new beginnings from time to time . . . even more missions."

As I left the mission field I prayed fervently and at length that this promise might be fulfilled. Thirty-four years later it was partially fulfilled when I was called to be the stake mission president of the East Millcreek Stake. President Harold B. Lee gave me a beautiful blessing as he set me apart. Three and a half years later, it was further realized when I was called to preside over the Northwestern States Mission.

Sacrifice or Blessing?

As we have listened to missionaries bear their testimonies, many have told us how they put aside dreams and plans for school and careers and accepted mission calls. Others who have been called to important Church assignments have set aside, to a large extent, their personal affairs to give the needed attention to the work of the Lord; and all have borne witness of the happiness and blessings they and their families have received.

In 1959, when I received my call to preside over the Northwestern States Mission, it came at a most inconvenient time. But both Sister Richards and I felt that if the Lord wanted us to go, then we should go.

Many of our friends, Church members and nonmembers, indicated that they felt we were making a real sacrifice. We felt otherwise. As President McKay set me apart, he promised me that it would be the happiest time of our lives—and it was, because our entire time was spent in serving our fellowmen. And we remembered the words of King Benjamin: "When ye are in the service of your fellow beings ye are only in the service of your God." (Mosiah 2:17.)

Why should we consider it a sacrifice to enjoy such happiness, growth, and development? Again I was grateful that my parents had taught me to live by the rule "Thy will be done—not mine."

The Difficult Case of Death

In many other ways, to accept the will of the Lord is ofttimes most difficult, such as in the case of the death of a loved one. Death is an important part of eternal life, yet we are never quite ready for the change. Not knowing when it will come, we properly fight to retain life for ourselves and for our loved ones.

We pray for the sick and administer to the afflicted. We implore the Lord to heal and extend life. Not all are healed even though great faith may be manifested. However, God has given us a promise that though a loved one may die, yet he or she shall live again through the atonement and resurrection of our Lord and Savior, Jesus Christ.

The loss of loved ones is a difficult experience that builds faith, courage, and humility, and we must all expect such experiences.

To obtain the desired happiness on this earth and in the world to come, we must steadfastly face trials and tribulations, regardless of the form they take, with the spirit of "Thy will be done—not mine."

The Savior again set the pattern in this respect. No martyr ever approached death with greater courage and dignity than did Jesus Christ, our Lord and Savior.

Accepting the Savior

Undoubtedly, the greatest evidence of one's righteousness is to accept Jesus Christ as our Savior and Redeemer without any qualifications. By loving the Lord, keeping His commandments, and serving our fellow beings, we are doing his will, and this will bring us great happiness and eternal life.

Parenthood

Home or Church?

In discussing matters relating to parenthood, the home, and the Church, frequently the question arises, "Which comes first, the home or the Church?" Elder John A. Widtsoe said that "neither one comes first. They are one." (*Evidences and Reconciliations,* ed. G. Homer Durham [Salt Lake City: Book-craft, 1960], p. 318.) Both the home and the Church are part of the gospel plan of salvation.

Our Father in heaven has permitted us, as parents, to be partners with Him in bringing His spirit children to this earth. What a blessed relationship!

President J. Reuben Clark said, "We are responsible for the mortal tabernacling of that spirit; and . . . the child . . . comes at the invitation, virtually, of them who beget it. . . . Yours is the responsibility to see that this tabernacled spirit loses no opportunity, through you, to prove his worthiness and righteousness in living through his second estate. . . . You parents cannot shift the responsibility to anyone else. . . . The Church cannot take over the responsibility which is yours to train your children. The Church can aid, and should be the greatest aid; and we are derelict if we do not, as Church members and as Church organizations, provide that assistance. But beyond the Church . . . is the family, and it is our responsibility as parents to see to it that we fully perform our duties in this respect." ("Children's Rights," *Church News*, February 1, 1975, p. 16.)

Marriage—a Partnership

Marriage is ordained of God for the advancement and protection of the family. In marriage a man and woman having the same purposes can bring together the powers and strengths of both for great accomplishments. When parents support and cooperate with one another, whether it be in the home, in the Church, in outside activities, or in the development of their talents, they are reinforced and go forth with strength, courage, and determination to accomplish their goals.

To make this partnership effective and complete, we need our Heavenly Father to be a part of it, helping to guide us in our plans and in the daily consummation of these plans. It is His Spirit that adds strength and purpose to all that we do.

Our Responsibility to Ourselves

I feel that as parents we have a responsibility not only to our children, but also to ourselves. We are charged with the responsibility of first saving our own souls. The Savior taught that the great commandment is to love the Lord and, then, to love our neighbors *as ourselves*. We have a responsibility to ourselves to develop our greatest potential, to live in such a way that we may be worthy to return and live with our Heavenly Father. However, these goals cannot be reached through a selfish concern for ourselves, but only as we serve our Heavenly Father and our fellowmen.

Our Responsibility to Our Children

In a good LDS home with which I am familiar, there is a plaque that reads: "Let us all watch over each other that we may sit down in heaven together."

Every child is entitled to three fundamental things: a respected name, a sense of security, and opportunities for development. There is no mention among these of a heritage of land or money or high social position.

A good, honorable name is something every man and woman should pass on to their children. The prophet Nephi said with pride, "I . . . [was] born of goodly parents." (1 Ne. 1:1.)

A sense of security comes to a child when he knows he is loved and is an important part of the family. Every act of affection and sharing of family duties and responsibilities reinforces it. The love of a father and mother for each other does much to make a child feel secure.

One of the important reasons for our coming to this earth is to develop physically, mentally, morally, and spiritually. It is the obligation of every home to give to its members every opportunity possible for this growth. Generally, parents are very careful to see that their children are given proper food, exercise, and everything needed for good physical growth. They make sacrifices to help their children receive an education, but are they just as diligent about helping them to have proper moral standards and ideals?

How to Give Children What They Need

Specifically, there are several things that we as parents should do to help our children.

We should set a good example.

We should hold regular family home evenings. We have been promised that as we do so, there will be more love and understanding among all members of the family. These blessings are vital to a family's welfare.

We should teach our children the importance of studying the scriptures.

We should teach our children the value of family and personal prayer. I have found there is truth in the slogan "Families that pray together stay together."

We should teach our children good work habits and the value of paying a full tithing on their income.

We should help our children to prepare for missions and temple marriage.

We should show our children how to be missionaries every day.

Sometimes we must discipline our children, but when we do, we should remember what the Lord has told us: "Reproving betimes with sharpness, when moved upon by the Holy Ghost; and then showing forth afterwards an increase of love toward him whom thou hast reproved, lest he esteem thee to be his enemy; that he may know that thy faithfulness is stronger than the cords of death." (D&C 121:43-44.)

We should recognize that we cannot live our children's lives, and even though we would sincerely desire that all of our children live the gospel principles completely, not all do so. You are all familiar with the beautiful parable of the Prodigal Son given us by our Lord and Savior. When the son returned home the father did not condemn him; rather, he prepared a feast and welcomed him home. (See Luke 15:11-24.) Yes, there should be great joy in a family when a member who has strayed from the good life repents and returns.

Heaven Begins at Home

We are told that the life hereafter will be beautiful beyond our comprehension. But to assure ourselves of such a wonderful future, there is much that we must do in this life. President David O. McKay counseled us to make our homes "a bit of heaven on earth" with all the love and concern and caring for one another that it takes to make them just that—a bit of heaven on earth.

I recall that President Stephen L Richards said, "One of the most beautiful principles of the gospel is the eternal nature of the family." Loving our children as we do, can any parents feel that it would be heaven if they didn't have their children with them?

As members of a family support each other, the Lord will bless them, and they will be able to take care of their family responsibilities and at the same time magnify their Church callings.

Patience

The Lord's Counsel

As the foundations of the Church were being laid in this dispensation, many wonderful revelations were given for the guidance of those engaged in the great work. Although some revelations were given to particular persons, we know that they were generally for the edification and direction of all who would heed them, whether at that time or at a later time.

One of the great revelations was given in February 1829 through the Prophet Joseph Smith to his father, and is recorded in section 4 of the Doctrine and Covenants. The revelation commences with the declaration that a marvelous work is about to come forth among the children of men. Qualities necessary for success in the Lord's service are then given and include faith, virtue, knowledge, temperance, and patience. (See D&C 4:6.)

In today's world of uncertainty, pressures, strains, and tribulations, patience is a very essential virtue. The dictionary definition of patience is: to be undisturbed by obstacles, delays, or failures, to be able to bear strain and stress, to be persevering, to possess the ability to exercise forbearance under provocation.

The Purpose of Patience

The Apostle Paul, in writing to the saints in Rome, said, "We glory in tribulations . . . knowing that tribulation worketh patience; and patience, experience; and experience, hope." (Rom. 5:3-4.)

And so our trials and tribulations, as we meet them with patience, give us valuable experiences and prepare us for challenges that lie ahead. All of life's experiences provide us with opportunities to develop patience.

Exercising Patience

In periods of health, prosperity, and well-being, many people are inclined to overlook the importance of patience and are apt to become impatient. It's not uncommon to overextend oneself physically, mentally, financially, or in many ways.

In 1828 the Lord, in a revelation to the Prophet Joseph Smith, said, "Do not run faster or labor more than you have strength." (D&C 10:4.)

By exercising patience, we will not be inclined to run faster or labor more than our strength justifies. In this regard, an adage that has been particularly helpful and inspirational to me is "Survey large fields but cultivate small ones." Often we want to cultivate large fields before we are properly prepared and equipped to do so. Concentrating on an immediate task while envisioning and planning for extensive growth requires genuine patience, and patience is essential to sound growth and development.

Some might construe patience to be a negative force that results in resignation and discouragement. However, it is a stabilizing influence, while impatience frequently brings fear, tension, discouragement, and failure.

In a revelation given through the Prophet Joseph Smith to his brother Hyrum in May 1829, the Lord counseled Hyrum in regard to his assignment, saying, "Be patient until you shall accomplish it." (D&C 11:19.) Here patience is identified as a positive force and as a requisite to accomplishment.

How to Develop Patience

One way to develop patience and to make it a positive force is to carefully plan our activities and set realistic objectives and goals. Sound planning requires meditation, patience, and prayer.

Frequently, patience is developed when it is coupled with repentance—a changing of one's attitude, a controlling of one's temper, or some other corrective action. Patience combined with prayer, repentance, faith, and works will help one overcome many kinds of obstacles.

Patience is closely related to persevering, and persevering means work—mental and physical.

When to Use Patience

To develop patience, don't expect too much too soon. Make the most of what you have.

Exercise patience in the matter of buying a new home, a new car, furniture, or other important things. Get out of debt and stay out of debt. Here patience will reward you with peace of mind, happiness, and success.

A young person should plan and patiently prepare for a mission years ahead of the time he leaves, providing he wants to perform an outstanding mission.

Planning for and obtaining an education are especially important in this day and age; and, of course, planning and preparing for a vocation are significant parts of one's goals in education. Faith and patience are vital to accomplish the desired objectives.

Hasty courtships tend to create unhappy marriages. Be patient in the selection of a husband or wife. Be patient and take sufficient time to prepare for temple marriage. Here is one area where your patience will be rewarded with eternal blessings.

Our greatest need for continual patience is with our loved ones, members of our family. Here is where we may be the most impatient, but here is where patience pays the greatest dividends. Nothing is sweeter than to watch a loving parent patiently teach his child the right way to do something. For example, a father stood beside his small son in a swimming pool. The boy wanted so much to learn to swim, and the father patiently showed him how. Day after day they returned to the pool, the father always evidencing patience and appreciation for the boy's efforts.

This same method is used by truly successful parents in teaching their children the lessons of life, telling and showing, over and over, until the lesson is learned—always with patience, love, and appreciation of every evidence of progress, no matter how small.

Patience in Church Work

Patience and perseverance in Church work also pay tremendous dividends.

As early as 1831, the Lord, in a revelation given to the Prophet Joseph Smith, counseled the elders of the Church to "be not weary in well-doing, for ye are laying the foundation of a great work. And out of small things proceedeth that which is great." (D&C 64:33.)

How important this counsel is to us today! Be patient in your home teaching and other teaching assignments, in your home evenings, and in all relationships with one another.

I recall that in our stake mission, missionaries called on one nonmember family at least once every three months over a period of two and a half years, but were never invited into the home. Then, on the next visit, they were invited in, and the family agreed to be taught the gospel. As they studied, prayed, and attended church, each member of the family received a testimony and was baptized. The reward of patiently persevering in this case was the bringing of an entire family into the kingdom of God.

As one reviews the various activities of life and the many human inadequacies that are evident, the value of patience becomes increasingly evident. Sometimes we are misunderstood even by those who are closest to us. Under such circumstances, patience will develop within us the capacity to accept criticism and censure, whether we feel such criticism is warranted or not. This ability to exercise forbearance under provocation means that we are following the Savior's teachings to do good to those who despitefully use us, and to turn the other cheek. (See Matt. 5:44, 39.)

Patience is truly a mighty virtue. It can be developed as each of us recognizes its importance and makes up his mind to be patient within his own life as well as with others. I encourage you to develop patience in your daily life and enjoy the satisfaction of accomplishment, free from many of the customary pressures and strains incident to modern living.

Perfecting the Saints

Reach Out to Inactives

To accomplish the perfecting of the Saints, The Church of Jesus Christ of Latter-day Saints provides opportunities for all members to become involved in many different kinds of activities that develop them mentally, morally, physically, and spiritually.

A high percentage of the members of the Church are active in the perfection process and are being blessed in many ways. There are, however, many inactive men who do not hold the Melchizedek Priesthood. These potential leaders are called prospective elders. We have a great challenge to bring these, our brothers, more actively into the perfection process.

President Spencer W. Kimball referred to this challenge in a talk in which he asked the members of the Church to lengthen their stride. He said, "The cycles of inactivity and indifference are recurring cycles from father to son. The Church must now break that cycle at two points simultaneously: We must reach out and hold many more of our young men of the Aaronic Priesthood to keep them faithful, to help them to be worthy to go on missions and to be married in the holy temple; we must, at the same time, reach and hold more of the fathers and the prospective holders of the Melchizedek Priesthood.

"We must find improved ways of vitalizing our Melchizedek Priesthood quorums, particularly in order to reach the prospective elders who are, in so many cases, the fathers of so many of our boys and girls and our young men and women." (Address to Regional Representatives, October 3, 1974.)

Why Are Some Inactive?

Why are these members inactive? I believe the main reasons are that they do not understand the gospel and they do not fully appreciate the blessings that come from Church activity.

What can be done to reduce the number of young men attaining the age of eighteen and not being ordained to the office of an elder? Let me give you a few suggestions and examples.

We must recognize that the programs of the Aaronic Priesthood quorums, the auxiliaries, the seminaries, and the institutes are playing a very important role in training these young men. However, their parents, their families, and all of us can also have tremendous influence in their lives.

The living example set by parents is consciously and unconsciously absorbed by children. Solomon, in his wisdom, has told us: "Train up a child in the way he should go: and when he is old, he will not depart from it." (Prov. 22:6.)

Some time ago, I stayed in the home of a stake president who had a young son nine years of age. I slept in this young man's bedroom, and I noticed on his dresser a little cardboard bank with three compartments—one for his tithing, one for his mission, and one for fun. I asked him if he was going on a mission, and he replied, "That's what I am saving my money for." I am sure that with this type of planning he will be worthy to be ordained an elder and will be prepared for missionary service.

In another stake president's home one weekend, I slept in another boy's room. There on the wall were pictures of all the temples. He was planning for a temple marriage as well as a mission.

Older children also have a great influence upon younger children. As I was interviewing a prospective missionary, I asked him, "Why do you want to go on a mission?" He replied. "I know this church is the Church of Jesus Christ, and I want to tell others about it. And besides, I'm the oldest child in our family, and I want to set a pattern for my brothers to follow." What a wonderful spirit!

What Reactivates Inactive Members?

Let us not forget that many stake presidents, bishops, high councilors, and quorum leaders at one time in their lives were inactive or prospective elders. What caused them to become involved again in the perfection process? Perhaps a few examples will point out some of the important reasons for their return.

A reactivated elder stood in a fast and testimony meeting and explained what it meant to have his firstborn child enter their home. "When I began to realize my responsibility to guide this wonderful little soul through life," he explained, "I knew that only by honoring the priesthood I had neglected could I be the kind of father I want to be."

A former prospective elder told me what it meant to him for the elders quorum president to ask him to serve as an assistant secretary in the elders quorum presidency. He took a week to decide to accept the assignment, but when he did, he marveled at the change that came into his life. He said, "Suddenly, I felt not only wanted, but actually needed."

We should involve prospective elders in Church activities even though at first their assignments may be minor. I recall listening to thrilling reports from prospective elders and new converts who were assigned to raise and lower the chapel flag each day, or to keep the song books in repair, or to assist quorum officers. In each instance, the persons involved were happy and had worthwhile experiences.

Testimony of a Happy Man

Let me share with you some of the feelings of a prospective elder who has recently come into full Church activity. He writes, "Returning to Church activity after years of absence would have been impossible without a lot of help. I'll always be grateful for that evening when my elders quorum president came to my home and said, 'Roger, starting next Sunday evening we are having two other couples over to our home once a week to talk about some important gospel principles. We would be pleased if you and Pat would join us.'

"I know it took courage for him to invite us, but that was an important beginning. That was the first time anyone had ever asked me to get back into Church activity. In those fireside meetings, my wife and I learned things about the gospel that we had never understood before. When testimonies were expressed, we felt feelings that had been dulled in many ways by inactivity.

"As we started having family prayer together, we felt a special spirit enter our home. Before long, I became so anxious to learn about the gospel that I found myself reading the scriptures on the bus going to and from work, and even during my noon hour."

His letter then tells the great joy he and his wife felt as they went to the temple, where they and their children were sealed together for time and all eternity. And now they are helping prepare their three sons for missionary service.

To you who are not now involved in Church activity, we extend our love and want you to know how eager we are to share with you the blessings of the priesthood and the gospel. There will never be a better time than now to become active in the process of self-protection. I promise you it will bring you peace, happiness, and joy along with growth and development.

Prayer

An Atmosphere of Peace

Prayer is an essential element in developing spirituality. The Savior instructed His disciples to pray always, saying, "Ask, and it shall be given you; seek, and ye shall find; knock, and it shall be opened unto you. For every one that asketh receiveth; and he that seeketh findeth; and to him that knocketh it shall be opened." (Luke 11:9-10.)

In an atmosphere of peace and communion with God, we keep in tune with the Holy Ghost. The life's pattern and life's teachings of the Savior incorporate prayer, love, service, and spiritual achievement.

The Vitality of Prayer

Implanted in the heart of every person born on this earth, regardless of his or her race or color, is the desire to worship in some manner a divine being.

The Prophet Joseph Smith observed that "it is the first principle of the gospel to know for a certainty the character of God, and to know that we may converse with Him as one man converses with another." (*History of the Church* 6:305.)

Further, "the Father has a body of flesh and bones as tangible as man's; the Son also; but the Holy Ghost has not a body of flesh and bones, but is a personage of Spirit." (D&C 130:22.)

Reflecting upon the fact that we can converse with God as

one man converses with another reminds us that we not only have a divine spark within us, but that we are actually spirit children of our Father in heaven. Throughout the ages the avenue of communication between man and God generally begins with prayer.

What Is Prayer?

Prayer, being the primary method of communication between God and man, plays an important part in almost every religion, whether Christian or otherwise. This is particularly true in The Church of Jesus Christ of Latter-day Saints.

People who become interested in Mormon doctrine are told to study, pray, and attend church. They are promised that if they do so, having faith in Christ, they will receive a testimony of its truthfulness.

Prayer is the "simplest form of speech," "the soul's sincere desire, uttered or unexpressed." (*Hymns*, no. 220.) Prayer is a period of quiet meditation, of self-examination, of confession of weakness. Prayer is fellowship with God.

Prayer opened the heavens to the Prophet Joseph Smith. It opened the dispensation of the fulness of times. The Church of Jesus Christ of Latter-day Saints is a monument to prayer.

Doing Our Part

Brigham Young stated: "You know that it is one peculiarity of our faith and religion never to ask the Lord to do a thing without being willing to help him all that we are able; and then the Lord will do the rest." (*Discourses of Brigham Young*, p. 43.)

"Please, Lord, help me to help myself." I am convinced that this prayer for increased personal power—spiritual strength, greater inspiration, and greater confidence—is one that God always answers. We can learn to solve our own problems with God's help, making him our partner.

The laws governing prayer are as immutable as those governing science. Response is predicated upon our living so that we are entitled to the whisperings of the Spirit. We must keep ourselves in tune with the Holy Ghost. After this, our part is to commit ourselves to act in conformity with the inspiration received. Then, as we do our part or magnify our calling, the Lord will make us equal to the task by blessing us with strength of body and of mind far beyond our normal capacities.

Some Practical Suggestions

What can we do to supplement prayer? What is our part? What does it mean to magnify a calling? Let me suggest a few examples.

As we pray for wisdom and knowledge, our part can be to study and apply ourselves.

As we pray for health and strength of body and of mind, our part can include living the Word of Wisdom.

As we pray for protection in our travels, our part would be to use good judgment, such as driving carefully if we are going by car.

When we pray for patience, our part would be to persevere and remember that the Lord has counseled us to "be not weary in well-doing, for . . . out of small things proceedeth that which is great." (D&C 64:33.)

When we pray for inspiration, our part is to live close to the Lord by keeping His commandments.

How to Pray

How should we pray? The Savior answered this question when He said: "After this manner therefore pray ye: Our Father which art in heaven, Hallowed be thy name. Thy kingdom come. Thy will be done in earth, as it is in heaven. Give us this day our daily bread. And forgive us our debts, as we forgive our debtors. And lead us not into temptation, but deliver us from evil: For thine is the kingdom, and the power, and the glory, for ever. Amen." (Matt. 6:9-13.)

This simple prayer envisions appreciation, simplicity, and the avoidance of vain repetitions. Let our prayers be our soul's sincere desire. In our church worship, there are only three set prayers—the baptismal and two sacramental prayers.

When to Pray

When should we pray? Generally, I think we should pray in secret, with our families, and in public assemblies.

Secret prayer should have a place in every person's life. Again the Savior gave us the pattern when He said, "When thou prayest, enter into thy closet, and when thou hast shut thy door, pray to thy Father which is in secret; and thy Father which seeth in secret shall reward thee openly." (Matt. 6:6.)

The Prophet Joseph Smith, speaking on this subject, stated, "We would say to the brethren, seek to know God in your closets, call upon him in the fields. Follow the directions in the Book of Mormon, and pray over, and for your families, your cattle, your flocks, your herds, your corn, and all things that you possess; ask the blessing of God upon all your labors, and everything that you engage in." (*History of the Church* 5:31.)

Family prayer should be a part of our daily worship. It should express our appreciation to our Father in heaven for our many blessings, as well as our love for Him. We should likewise ask for our daily needs, as the Savior did in His prayer to the Father. The holding of family prayer is a powerful influence for good in every home where it is a regular practice. Morning and evening prayers, as well as the blessing on our food, bring us a sense of closeness to our Father in heaven, which is a stabilizing influence in our life.

President John Taylor asked the Saints, "Do you have prayers in your family? . . . And when you do, do you go through the operation like the grinding of a piece of machinery, or do you bow in meekness and with a sincere desire to seek the blessing of God upon you and your household? That is the way that we ought to do, and cultivate a spirit of devotion and trust in God, dedicating ourselves to him and seeking his blessings." (*The Gospel Kingdom,* ed. G. Homer Durham [Deseret Book, 1944], p. 284.)

The Lord has charged us to "teach [our] children to pray, and to walk uprightly before the Lord." (D&C 68:28.)

President Heber J. Grant, in referring to this matter, said, "I have little or no fear for the boy or girl, the young man or the young woman, who honestly and conscientiously supplicates God twice a day for the guidance of His Spirit. I am sure that when temptation comes they will have the strength to overcome it by the inspiration that shall be given to them." (*Gospel Standards,* comp. G. Homer Durham [Salt Lake City: Improvement Era, 1941], p. 26.)

As parents, we clearly have a duty and a privilege to teach our children to pray, and regular family prayers set the pattern.

Prayers Shared with Others

Public prayers are a part of our worship services and many other public gatherings. These prayers again put us in a frame of mind to be inspired, strengthened, and motivated.

Our sacramental and baptismal prayers are a very important part of our worship services.

Another valuable area of prayer is in administering to the sick. The Lord has made provision for this by having the elders of the Church administer to the sick, and this includes the exercise of the faith of all interested persons.

Healing the Disease of Fear

One of the most potent and devastating tools of the evil power is doubt and fear placed in the hearts of men. Actually, I feel that it is one of the major illnesses suffered by mankind. Prayer with faith and works on our part will definitely heal the dread disease of fear. It is a tremendous reactivating force, stimulating and refreshing the mind as well as the body. However, it is self-evident that one will never get the benefits derived from prayer unless he prays. Let us remember that God is no respecter of persons. He has promised to show mercy and to give comfort and strength to all who love him and keep His commandments. (See Acts 10:34-35.)

And let us remember that our attitude and approach should be similar to that of the Savior's in one of His last prayers in which He said, "Father, if thou be willing, remove this cup from me: nevertheless not my will, but thine, be done." Three times He prayed in this manner. "And there appeared an angel unto him from heaven, strengthening him." (Luke 22:42-43.)

May we commit ourselves to so live that we may go before the Lord with a clear conscience and ask for His divine guidance and assistance.

Reactivation

Wisdom, Key to Happiness

One of the great challenges facing us today is to develop sufficient wisdom, understanding, and inner strength so that we can live happily and successfully in our complex and difficult world and not be caught up in the mad scramble for material possessions and pleasures.

Recently two young people and one older man came to me and explained that, although each is successful in a material way, they are unhappy and confused. Each asked my advice as to how he could remedy his situation. I told them that the Lord had already answered that question when he said, "Seek not for riches but for wisdom, and behold, the mysteries of God shall be unfolded unto you, and then shall you be made rich. Behold, he that hath eternal life is rich." (D&C 6:7.)

I suggested that they probably needed to change their priorities in life and seek after wisdom rather than after so many material things and pleasures.

Work with Groups

President Spencer W. Kimball has asked us to lengthen our stride. One effective way to lengthen our stride is to start working with prospective elders. One thing that most of these inactive brethren have in common is that they do not know the doctrine of the Church. If they did, most of them would be active.

In my experience, I have found that many prospective elders have nonmember wives. In such cases, it would be appropriate for the elders quorum president to ask the ward mission leader to have the stake or full-time missionaries teach the nonmember wives with the cooperation and in the presence of the inactive husbands. Of course, the home teachers should continue the fellowshipping of these families.

In order to teach and reactivate larger numbers, I have found that teaching and fellowshipping in groups is most effective—in cottage meetings, so to speak. I have also experienced better results when working with groups that are compatible insofar as their age, education, and interests are concerned.

The Need for Study

This missionary approach should be one of our major efforts in accomplishing our objectives, particularly as study is so vital in obtaining a knowledge of the gospel and in seeking wisdom. The Lord has told us to "teach one another words of wisdom; yea, seek . . . out of the best books words of wisdom: seek learning, even by study and also by faith." (D&C 88:118.)

Great emphasis should be given to teaching prospective elders the doctrines of the Church. Excellent results have been achieved by many elders quorums in teaching temple project groups. Inasmuch as many of the prospective elders are older men, some elders quorums have used high priests successfully in the reactivation process. I can also envision groups participating in athletic events, square dancing, and many other recreational activities, all a part of the great reactivation program.

Involve the Inactives

Make certain that prospective elders and new converts have opportunities to become involved in Church activities.

It might be interesting to note that frequently, even when we seek after wisdom rather than riches, the Lord blesses us with wisdom and riches as he did King Solomon. When this occurs, we have the great opportunity and responsibility to use our material wealth in the building up of the kingdom of God.

Relationship to God

A Personal God

The first statement in the declaration of belief of The Church of Jesus Christ of Latter-day Saints is "We believe in God, the Eternal Father, and in His Son, Jesus Christ, and in the Holy Ghost." (Article of Faith 1.)

Belief in God is the life-giving element of the Church. Our conception of God is personal. God in this dispensation has revealed Himself to mankind as He did in former dispensations.

Through faith and prayer, Joseph Smith, as a young man, gained the great blessing of beholding God the Father and His Son Jesus Christ. In his own words, Joseph Smith said, "I saw two Personages, whose brightness and glory defy all description, standing above me in the air. One of them spake unto me, calling me by name and said, pointing to the other—*This is My Beloved Son. Hear Him!*" (Joseph Smith–History 1:17.)

The Gospel Plan

"Through the Atonement of Christ, all mankind may be saved, by obedience to the laws and ordinances of the Gospel." (Article of Faith 3.)

The Savior said, "Let not your heart be troubled: ye believe in God, believe also in me. . . . I am the way, the truth, and the life: no man cometh unto the Father, but by me." (John 14: 1, 6.)

Jesus taught that all the law and the prophets rests upon the principle of loving God with all of our heart, might, mind, and strength, and our neighbors as ourselves. The gospel of Jesus Christ is the plan of life that will restore peace to the world, remove inner tensions and troubles, and bring happiness and contentment—the greatest philosophy of life ever given to man.

The Gospel's Simplicity

The gospel is founded upon the basic principles of love of God and man and showing this love in service to our fellowmen. All mankind must shape their lives upon the simple principles He taught and lived in order to comprehend Him in His power and majesty.

King Benjamin, a great prophet, stated, "And behold, I tell you these things that ye may learn wisdom; that ye may learn that when ye are in the service of your fellow beings ye are only in the service of your God." (Mosiah 2:17.)

The Divine Spark

It is not unusual to hear a religious leader, a philosopher, or a poet refer to man as having a divine spark within him. Such characterizations imply that man possesses great abilities and potential. We are frequently admonished to develop our capabilities, reach out, and set high goals for ourselves.

What does it mean to have a divine spark within us? It means that man has a certain relationship with God. From time to time throughout the history of the world God has made known to man what this relationship is. The scriptures teach that God is a personal being in whose image man was created and that God the Father is the literal father of our Lord and Savior Jesus Christ and the father of the spirits of all men. Because of this, we inherit divine attributes. This was beautifully stated in the book of Job: "There is a spirit in man: and the inspiration of the Almighty giveth them understanding." (Job 32:8.)

This simple doctrine as taught by Christ gave way to the theories and dogmas of men through the hundreds of years of apostasy.

Our Understanding Restored

The Church of Jesus Christ of Latter-day Saints proclaims to the world that the gospel of Jesus Christ in its fulness and simplicity has been restored through the instrumentality of the Prophet Joseph Smith. We assert that God the Father and His Son Jesus Christ appeared to Joseph Smith and that Christ's church has been reestablished on the earth.

Thus, through modern revelation, God's relationship to man has again been clarified. The life of our earthly body is our spirit, and God the Eternal Father is the father of our spirit.

The apostle John testified that Jesus "was the true Light, which lighteth every man that cometh into the world." (John 1:9.) And in this dispensation President Joseph F. Smith bore witness to this same truth—that the light of Christ, the Spirit of Truth, "lighteth every man" who is born into the world.

What a tremendous effect this has in the lives of those who accept this doctrine! Our Father in heaven loves each and every one of us and is interested in our welfare and growth and development. In fact, His work and glory is "to bring to pass the immortality and eternal life of man." (Moses 1:39.)

With this relationship to our Heavenly Father, we are thus blessed with many talents and possess great possibilities. The Savior set our greatest goal for us when he said, "Be ye therefore perfect, even as your Father which is in heaven is perfect." (Matt. 5:48.)

Progress Is Our Responsibility

To become perfect requires growth and development; and as we contemplate perfection, we recognize that growth is the greatest phenomenon of this existence. The scriptures clearly emphasize our obligations to use and develop the gifts and talents we have been blessed with—shall we say, develop the spark of divinity within us? Human experience confirms the soundness of this doctrine.

Resurrection

The Easter Reminder

Easter time is a forceful reminder that the human spirit cannot be confined. It does not deny the reality of death, but it offers us an assurance that God has preserved life beyond the grave. It is interesting to note that the restored gospel as taught by The Church of Jesus Christ of Latter-day Saints encompasses belief in a literal resurrection, which is radically different from the concept taught by most Christian churches.

President Heber J. Grant often told how several hundred ministers were asked, "Do you believe that after you die you will live again as a conscious entity, knowing and being known as you are?" No doubt all of these ministers had conducted Easter services; but in answering, none actually believed in a literal resurrection.

Do Not Reject the Unexplained

It seems to be the nature of people to not accept things they cannot explain, and no one can explain the resurrection. Neither can one explain how life came to be, but who denies that we live? If we gave up everything that we cannot explain, we would have to give up life. But He who has given us life has assured us of life hereafter. Which is more difficult, to be born or to rise again? That we should live forever is no greater miracle than that we should live at all.

Throughout the centuries, philosophies and theories have been advanced by men relative to the resurrection, but none have seemed to satisfy the hearts and minds of honest searchers of truth.

The Gospel Answer of Birth and Death

The restored gospel of Jesus Christ explains that we existed as spirit entities before being born into this sphere of activity—yes, spirit children of our Father in heaven. We came to this earth for our spirits to receive bodies of flesh and bones and to have experiences, to see if we would do all things that the Lord should command us.

Birth and death in this world are steps in eternal life, birth being a transition from our preexistent state to this earth life, and death being a transition into the next sphere of activity. At death the spirit leaves our earthly body until the morning of the resurrection.

Through modern revelation we learn that "the spirit and the body are the soul of man. And the resurrection from the dead is the redemption of the soul. And the redemption of the soul is through him that quickeneth all things." (D&C 88: 15-17.)

Results of the Fall

As a result of the Fall, Adam and Eve suffered the penalty of spiritual and physical death. But, as Adam said, "Blessed be the name of God, for because of my transgression my eyes are opened, and in this life I shall have joy, and again in the flesh I shall see God.

"And Eve, his wife, heard all these things and was glad, saying: Were it not for our transgression we never should have had seed, and never should have known good and evil, and the joy of our redemption, and the eternal life which God giveth unto all the obedient." (Moses 5:10-11.)

The Fall thus provided a means whereby mankind can choose between good and evil and thus prepare for life after death. What we do here, then, determines to a considerable extent what we will be doing in the life after death. The Lord has told us that "whatever principle of intelligence we attain unto in this life, it will rise with us in the resurrection. And if a person gains more knowledge and intelligence in this life through his diligence and obedience than another, he will have so much the advantage in the world to come." (D&C 130:18-19.)

Christ's Sacrifice

It was Christ's right to be the Redeemer of mankind, and though it required sacrifice beyond our comprehension, He made the sacrifice voluntarily. He said, "Therefore doth my Father love me, because I lay down my life, that I might take it again. No man taketh it from me, but I lay it down of myself. I have power to lay it down, and I have power to take it up again. This commandment have I received of my Father." (John 10:17-18.)

The Savior had a consuming desire to do His Father's will, and He had great love for his Father's children, whose Redeemer He became. Thus, He not only atoned for Adam's transgression, but for the sins of all mankind. However, we must remember that redemption from individual sins depends upon individual effort.

Reality of the Resurrection

Matthew relates that "the graves were opened; and many bodies of the saints which slept arose, and came out of the graves after [the Savior's] resurrection, and went into the holy city, and appeared unto many." (Matt. 27:52-53.)

Today the resurrection is real to us for similar reasons. Christ and some of the ancient saints have appeared in this dispensation as resurrected beings. From a revelation to the Prophet Joseph Smith we learn that "there are two kinds of beings in heaven, namely: Angels, who are resurrected personages, having bodies of flesh and bones—For instance, Jesus said: *Handle me and see, for a spirit hath not flesh and bones, as ye see me have.* Secondly: the spirits of just men made perfect, they who are not [yet] resurrected, but inherit the same glory." (D&C 129:1-3.)

That Christ's resurrection was truly a reality was clearly demonstrated in this dispensation in Joseph Smith's first vision, when he saw two Personages, God the Father and His Son, Jesus Christ. (Joseph Smith–History 1:17.)

This testimony was again given by Joseph Smith in a vision to him and Sidney Rigdon wherein Joseph relates, "And now, after the many testimonies which have been given of him, this is the testimony, last of all, which we give of him: That he lives! For we saw him, even on the right hand of God; and we heard the voice bearing record that he is the Only Begotten of the Father—that by him, and through him, and of him, the worlds are and were created, and the inhabitants thereof are begotten sons and daughters unto God." (D&C 76:22-24.)

The Savior appeared to Joseph Smith as He did to the apostles in the upper room when He invited them to handle Him and see, lest they think Him to be a spirit. He said, "A spirit hath not flesh and bones, as ye see me have." (Luke 24:39.)

Yes, the message of Easter time is that Christ is alive today, that many of the Saints have been resurrected, and that all persons will enjoy a literal resurrection of the earthly body with the spirit.

Conditional Salvation

Ancient and modern scriptures make it clear that all persons will be resurrected, but only those who accept Jesus Christ and His gospel and keep His commandments will receive the greater blessings of eternal salvation.

The Savior has indicated that "all the dead [shall] awake, for their graves shall be opened, and they shall come forth—yea, even all. And the righteous shall be gathered on my right hand unto eternal life; and the wicked on my left hand will I be ashamed to own before the Father." (D&C 29:26-27.)

The Purpose of Life

One can see the significance and purpose of this life with the perspective the gospel plan gives. The restored gospel gives us an understanding of where we came from; of the importance of birth, death, and a literal resurrection of our earthly body; and of where we will go after this life.

The Lord has said, "If you keep my commandments and endure to the end you shall have eternal life, which gift is the greatest of all the gifts of God." (D&C 14:7.) With the understanding of the gospel that we have, may we all work for eternal life.

Reverence

"In the Beauty of Holiness"

The Psalmist said, "Give unto the Lord the glory due unto his name; worship the Lord in the beauty of holiness." (Ps. 29:2.) What a beautiful scripture and how full of direction! What does it mean to "worship the Lord in the beauty of holiness"? Let us examine this interesting challenge.

First, the Savior has repeatedly stated that His house is a house of order. In the early days of the restored Church, in a revelation to the Prophet Joseph Smith, the Lord emphasized this in saying, "Behold, mine house is a house of order, saith the Lord God, and not a house of confusion." (D&C 132:8.)

The Savior, when on earth, evidenced real indignation when He saw the temple being desecrated. He ordered those out who were causing the desecration and said, "Make not my Father's House an house of merchandise." (John 2:16.) It is the height of rudeness and disrespect to desecrate our houses of worship in any way, physically or by disturbance.

The dictionary defines *worship* as "the act of paying divine honor to Deity; religious reverence and homage." *Reverence* is "honor or respect felt or manifested; profound respect mingled with love and awe."

Worship in Holy Places

Worship of God is a vital part of our religious concepts. In our worship services, we "give unto the Lord the glory due unto his name"; we learn of God and the things He wants us to do; and we participate in sacred ordinances. We are inspired, strengthened, motivated, and comforted.

President David O. McKay had this to say about "worshipping the Lord in the beauty of holiness":

"Reverence is profound respect mingled with love. It is a 'complex emotion made up of mingled feelings of the soul.' Carlyle says it is 'the highest of human feelings.' . . .

"Churches are dedicated and set apart as houses of worship. This means that all who enter do so, or at least pretend to do so, with an intent to get nearer the presence of the Lord than they can in the street or amidst the worries of a workaday life. In other words, we go to the Lord's house to meet him and to commune with him in spirit. Such a meeting place, then, should first of all be fitting and appropriate in all respects, whether God is considered as the invited guest, or the worshipers as his guests.

"Whether the place of meeting is a humble chapel or a 'poem in architecture,' built of white marble and inlaid with precious stones makes little or no difference in our approach and attitude toward the Infinite Presence. To know that God is there should be sufficient to impel us to conduct ourselves orderly, reverently." (*Man May Know for Himself* [Deseret Book, 1967], pp. 26-27.)

Good order in our houses of worship contributes to the proper spirit of the speaker and to the quality of his message. A speaker is expected to prepare a message for those he speaks to, and he is entitled to an attentive audience. A prepared speaker not only receives inspiration from the Spirit, but he also responds to the condition of the audience.

Leaders Must Be Prepared

Planning and properly organizing are essential to reverent worship. This means that all details of a meeting must be arranged prior to the time the meeting is to start. This, of course, includes the making of necessary assignments. General Authorities, stake presidencies, bishoprics, and other leaders should set the example in being prepared and well-organized. We need strong leaders to set the pattern of discipline, as the principle of self-control is the basis of order and reverence. When proper preparation has been made prior to a meeting, reverent worship becomes easier.

One Bishopric's Suggestions

Upon the completion of our new chapel, our bishopric made some excellent suggestions on how to improve reverence and worship. I would like to mention a few of these.

Develop the habit of reverence in entering the chapel. All of us like to meet friends, and within our ward and stake, we all have many friends. There is nothing more natural than speaking to people we know, love, and admire when we meet them. Within the meetinghouse, however, there are foyers and other spaces similar to a fine living room. Develop the habit of visiting in those places, and then enter the chapel area for one purpose: to worship our Father in heaven.

Greet friends in the chapel with a smile instead of words.

Make it a habit to arrive a few minutes ahead of the scheduled meeting, and listen quietly to the prelude music. Proper organ music sets a mood of contemplation and worship.

The bishopric should be on the stand a few minutes prior to meeting time and invite other ward and stake leaders to do the same. A good rule to remember is less talking on the stand.

The selection of appropriate hymns and participation of leaders in the singing are important factors in reverential worship.

Teaching Children about Reverence

Teach children to sit quietly in the chapel and not enter and leave as the whim may dictate. The Lord loves children and intends that they should attend sacrament meeting. The partaking of the sacrament, the lessons, and the instructions they receive there are part of His plan. For small children and babies, cry rooms should be provided and should be used if the little ones are disturbing others.

Order and reverence should be taught in the home, preferably in family home evening, as well as in the Primary. The trouble generally starts when children begin to mix with the older folks and see how disorderly and disrespectful they frequently are. Order and reverence, therefore, should be taught to young and old alike. This necessarily must be a continual process of education and training at all levels of Church administration.

Families should sit together during sacrament meetings. This is the program of the Church, and there is real merit in following it to develop reverent worship.

Our Father's house is a house of order. Good ushering contributes to orderliness, and this is a service that can be properly handled by the Aaronic Priesthood.

Foyers and hallways are not the places to be when meetings are going on in the chapel. Youths sometimes find it convenient to lounge in those places during meeting time. This does not contribute to reverent worship and should not be permitted.

Every officer and teacher shares in the privilege and responsibility to create an atmosphere in which reverence can increase.

Respecting Church Buildings and Grounds

Often reverence for the house of the Lord is interpreted only in terms of being quiet and respectful while we are in our chapels. But it should go further than that. Our buildings inside and out should be maintained properly and the grounds well kept.

The Church, to a large extent, is judged by the appearance of its buildings and grounds. The grounds should be planted and landscaped. The lawns should be watered and cut regularly and the shrubs properly trimmed. Do we keep the grounds around our chapels looking as good as those around our own homes? They should be places of distinction of which we can be proud.

Buildings should be protected properly against fire and vandalism, and parents and teachers should teach children to avoid vandalism or desecration of Church property. It is reported that a schoolhouse in Weissenburg, Germany, had been used eighteen months by four hundred children without a visible mar or scratch anywhere, from the entrance to the restrooms. When asked how a building could be kept in such perfect condition, the custodian said, "It is the mothers. The mothers teach the children not to destroy or deface public property."

Strict discipline of children is a necessary part of their normal development. If a child is allowed to disturb a meeting, destroy books, or mar a building, he learns that it is his privilege to do so.

The Chapel in Palmer, Alaska

I remember visiting our branch in Palmer, Alaska, several years ago. This lovely little building was beautifully maintained. Everything inside and outside the building was in perfect order. Upon inquiry, I learned that there was no paid custodian, but that one family was assigned each month to maintain the building and grounds. This family was to perform all custodial functions for the month assigned.

The family taking care of the building and grounds when we

were there reported that all of their children assisted them, and at Primary, when a neighbor boy was about to mark the wall of the classroom with a crayon, the little son of the responsible family grabbed the other little boy and said, "You can't do that! We have to keep the building clean this month."

We should teach all our members to have pride in the appearance of our buildings and to sense their responsibility to maintain their beauty as this little boy sensed his. If cleanliness is next to godliness, our chapels should be kept spotless and in perfect order.

The Blessings of Orderly Worship

Reverent worship evidences our love of God and increases our desire to keep His commandments. As a part of this worship, we learn the will of the Lord, our minds and hearts are touched, and our testimonies are strengthened. As we put ourselves in tune with the Spirit of the Lord, the Holy Ghost can guide and direct through inspiration. As the apostle Paul wrote to the Galatians, "The fruit of the Spirit is love, joy, peace, longsuffering, gentleness, goodness, faith, meekness, temperance: against such there is no law." (Gal. 5:22-23.)

Through reverent worship we become the recipients of inspiration, comfort, strength, and motivation to become perfect even as our Father in heaven is perfect.

These blessings are very much worthwhile, and are they not the blessings our Father in heaven desires for us when we "worship the Lord in the beauty of holiness"?

Sacrifice

The Surrenders of Sacrifice

Webster's Dictionary defines sacrifice as "a surrender of some desirable thing for a higher object." This is undoubtedly true, but it might be observed that the higher object is not always discernible at the time the surrender or sacrifice is made.

However, to fully realize the importance of the law of sacrifice, it is necessary to consider the purpose of life. This earth life has been provided that each of us might be proved to see if we will do all things that the Lord commands us to do.

While the Lord has given us a clear plan to follow, we must recognize that evil influences exist and provide temptations and obstacles for us to overcome. As Lehi said to his son Jacob, "It must needs be, that there is an opposition in all things. If not so, . . . righteousness could not be brought to pass." (2 Ne. 2:11.)

Inasmuch, then, as this earth life is a proving ground, it provides choices for us, and frequently the decisions we have to make are not easy. Many of our decisions require sacrifice, and sacrifice involves giving up something—something that may appear important and desirable.

Sacrifice—a Fundamental Law

The law of sacrifice is a fundamental doctrine of the gospel of Jesus Christ and contributes to the building of faith, love, victory, and glory.

In considering our free agency and the opposition that exists in all things, we must never forget that God always functions within eternal laws. The Lord has said, "I, the Lord, am bound when ye do what I say; but when ye do not what I say, ye have no promise" (D&C 82:10), and that "when we obtain any blessing from God, it is by obedience to that law upon which it is predicated" (D&C 130:21).

The Savior also said, "Let no man be afraid to lay down his life for my sake; for whoso layeth down his life for my sake shall find it again." (D&C 103:27.) Thus, the supreme sacrifice of one's life is rewarded by that person's finding his own life again, "even life eternal." (D&C 98:13.)

You and I may never be asked to lay down our lives for the gospel's sake, but obedience to the law of sacrifice in a lesser way is also rewarding.

The Blessings of Sacrifice

The inspiring hymn "Praise to the Man" asserts that "sacrifice brings forth the blessings of heaven." (Hymns, no. 147.) About the time this hymn was written, the Saints were experiencing many blessings resulting from their manifold sacrifices. The Prophet impressed upon them this truth when he said, "A religion that does not require the sacrifice of all things never has power sufficient to produce the faith necessary unto life and salvation. . . . It was through this sacrifice, and this only, that God has ordained that men should enjoy eternal life." (Lectures on Faith 6:7.)

Giving All That We Have

President Lorenzo Snow, one of the prophets of this dispensation, in speaking to the Saints in 1898, said: "We have found the treasure in the field, we have found the Pearl of Great Price—and now we have got to give all that we have for it—at one time or another. The Lord has said that he will prove us, even unto death, to see whether we will stand by the covenant we have made with him."

We are told plainly and unequivocally that our greatest opportunity and responsibility here is building the kingdom of God, Christ's church on earth. I know this to be true!

Elder Lyman's Counsel

In 1894, Elder Francis M. Lyman of the Council of the Twelve gave this counsel:

"It will be profitable to all Latter-day Saints to make this Church first in their hearts and affections. Why? Because the Lord has told us to seek first the kingdom of God. We have sought the kingdom and have found it—and now that should have our attention before farming, before merchandising, and before literary pursuits and the like.

"The welfare of the Church of Christ in the earth and the spreading abroad of the gospel should be our primary object.

"But is this the case with us? If it is not, then we have need of reformation. If the Church of Christ and the principles of righteousness are not foremost in our hearts, then I say all Israel so far as they lack have need of reformation.

"If we have set our hearts upon property, whether it be little or much (for I presume a man could worship a little property as well as a great deal,) then we are idolators, and God has forbidden us to be idolators. He has commanded us not to bow down to worship anything on earth."

This counsel is as important and applicable today as it was when it was given—perhaps more so.

Learning and Experience

How much learning and how many experiences do we need to become godlike? The answer to that is that we need all we can receive on this earth, and as we successfully meet this life's challenges, we will be prepared for more as we leave this estate and move into the next estate in the hereafter.

Our Father has sent us here for a short period of mortal experience. He has given us principles to guide us and has endowed us with free agency to choose our paths. As we choose the right, we are promised eternal progress and love and peace with our families and friends. And He has promised us that as we keep His commandments, His Spirit will be with us.

Words cannot describe the happiness that comes into our lives when the Spirit of God is with us. This happiness includes peace that passeth understanding except to the person who receives it. Let us truly appreciate the object of this life and endure to the end by meeting life's challenges with a determination to make each experience of eternal value to us and thus a contribution to our eternal progress.

Not Sacrifice—Opportunity!

Sometimes we may think that we have too many opportunities to serve and develop our talents, and we may feel that it requires too much of a sacrifice. Let me suggest, however, that we do not consider these opportunities as requiring sacrifices, but rather as opportunities to grow and develop and receive blessings.

I am confident that in every area of life's activities there are more opportunities awaiting the young leaders of today than any generation heretofore. I have great faith in our young men and women of today.

Our Heavenly Father has blessed each one of us with talents. He has told us so. Your talents may be different from your brother's or sister's or a friend's, but you have them. You must find out what they are and develop them, that they might bring joy and happiness into your own life and the lives of others.

Christ's Example of Sacrifice

Jesus' life was the perfect example of dedication and sacrifice. He had no silver or gold to give, but he gave faith to his disciples, health to the sick, and hope to the discouraged. His life was in every respect a sacrifice for all.

Joseph Smith's life was another great example of dedication and sacrifice. While in Liberty Jail the word of the Lord came to him: "If thou shouldst be cast into the pit, or into the hands of murderers, and the sentence of death passed upon thee, . . . know thou, my son, that all these things shall give thee experience, and shall be for thy good." (D&C 122:7.)

Here the Prophet was specifically told that these tribulations and sacrifices would be for his good and blessing, and undoubtedly the Liberty Jail experience was preparing him for coming events. In the end, he and his brother Hyrum were called upon to be martyrs for the kingdom of God—another great story of sacrifice and blessing.

The Rich Young Ruler and the Apostles

On one occasion, a rich young ruler came to the Savior and asked what he should do to be saved. Jesus enumerated several things, including honoring his parents, chastity, and honesty. The young man replied that he had done all of these things from his youth. Then Jesus told him to go and sell all that he had, give it to the poor, and follow Him. But the young man thought more of his riches than the kingdom, and he refused to make this sacrifice. (See Mark 10:17-22.)

On another occasion, one of Jesus' disciples indicated that he wanted to follow Him, but said, "Lord, suffer me first to go and bury my father." Jesus replied, "Follow me; and let the dead bury their dead." (Matt. 8:21-22.)

As the Savior was calling the fisherman Simon, also called Peter, and other disciples, He said, "Fear not; from henceforth thou shalt catch men." Then the record adds these significant words: "When they had brought their ships to land, they forsook all, and followed him." (Luke 5:10-11.)

Peter and the other disciples were willing to accept and comply with the law of sacrifice. The rich young ruler was not. According to the dictionary definition, Peter and the other disciples were willing to surrender a desirable condition for a higher object; the rich young ruler was not. Peter and the other disciples received the blessings.

The Need for Greater Dedication

As I travel throughout the Church, I am told by the leaders that the most pressing need today is for greater dedication on the part of everyone in building the kingdom. In Jesus' parables, we are told that the price of possessing the hidden treasure and the pearl of great price is one's all—complete dedication. We might ask, "How does the Lord interpret 'giving our all' or 'complete dedication,' and how will he prove us even unto death?"

Giving our all, or complete dedication, means putting the Church first in our lives. It means accepting every opportunity to serve. As you accept each call, recognize the tremendous opportunity even though the assignment may not appear to be too important or you may feel inadequate.

Opportunities to serve in building the kingdom are varied and many. Some require giving of our time; others require giving of our talents, and others, of our means. When we accept any assignment to serve, "giving our all" means giving all of the time, talents, and means necessary to accomplish the righteous objective.

Giving Our All

Few are asked to lay down their lives in building the kingdom; but if this were to be required, we should be willing to do so. In many respects, it is better to live for the Church than to die for it. Living for the Church can mean accepting a call as a teacher, a quorum or auxiliary leader, a bishop, a stake officer, a temple or welfare worker, a home teacher, a missionary, or in performing any service for our fellowmen.

The Church of Jesus Christ of Latter-day Saints has no paid ministry. Bishops of the wards, for example, are laymen and arrange their time and affairs so that they can provide and care for their families and still shepherd the flocks over which they are placed. This type of service is truly giving one's all.

Giving our all involves contributing financially to the growth and development of the kingdom.

He who pays an honest tithe and makes his other offerings as required is giving his all. The widow's mite is as acceptable as the rich man's abundance.

Taking care of the poor and needy through welfare projects and in many other ways requires the giving of our means, as does the building of chapels, temples, schools, and other church buildings in order to care for the spiritual and physical needs of God's children. Many throughout the world have left their homes, much like the missionaries, to serve in the vast building program of the Church. Substantial financial contributions as well as time are required to carry on the worldwide building operation.

Sacrifice brings forth the blessings of heaven, and in this respect financial sacrifice means opportunities for great and varied blessings. Certainly the sacrifice entailed in contributing financially to the building of the kingdom is an outstanding example of giving one's all.

Giving with the Right Attitude

The apostle Paul, in writing to the Corinthian saints, emphasized the importance of our attitude in giving when he said: "He which soweth sparingly shall reap also sparingly; and he which soweth bountifully shall reap also bountifully. Every man according as he purposeth in his heart, so let him give; not grudgingly, or of necessity: for God loveth a cheerful giver." (2 Cor. 9:6-7.)

Jesus, in teaching his disciples, counseled, "Lay not up for yourselves treasures upon earth, where moth and rust doth corrupt, and where thieves break through and steal: But lay up for yourselves treasures in heaven, where neither moth nor rust doth corrupt, and where thieves do not break through nor steal: For where your treasure is, there will your heart be also." (Matt. 6:19-21.)

The message of Christianity is to love and to serve, and we truly show our love by our good works. To attain real greatness, the Savior tells us, one must be the servant of all. (See Matt. 20:27.)

Are We as Dedicated Today as Before?

The question is frequently asked, Are people as dedicated today in building the kingdom as they were in former times? I feel that generally they are.

Giving our all today may, in some respects, be different than heretofore, but I see evidences every day where men, women, and children are showing their love of God and their fellowmen by their complete dedication. They are gladly giving their all in time, talents, and means. I commend them for it. I counsel all others to put the Church first in their lives and reap the peace, happiness, and contentment that come from giving their all through complete dedication.

Each period of the past had its own peculiar tests, and as they were successfully met, a broad and solid foundation was laid for us to build upon. We are living in a new era, a period of constant changes, a time of unprecedented growth and development. Our problems are those incident to rapid growth and change. Far-reaching challenges are requiring the sacrifice of the Saints—sacrifices possibly as great as ever before.

Sacrifices today are, in reality, opportunities, as they have always been. With reference to sacrifices incurred in building the kingdom of God, the Savior promised, "There is no man that hath left house, or parents, or brethren, or wife, or children, for the kingdom of God's sake, who shall not receive manifold more in this present time, and in the world to come life everlasting." (Luke 18:29-30.) How true this is!

Each of us has his duties to perform; and to perform them faithfully should be our constant aim, even though self-denial is required. May we each put the Church first in our lives and more fully understand and appreciate the eternal laws of sacrifice and work. May these virtues become a part of our daily lives, that we and our families may enjoy the blessings derived therefrom.

Scripture Study

Study the Standard Works

As this dispensation opened, the Lord instructed the elders of the Church in this manner: "And I give unto you a commandment that . . . ye shall teach [the scriptures] unto all men; for they shall be taught unto all nations, kindreds, tongues, and people. Thou shalt take the things which thou hast received, which have been given unto thee in my scriptures for a law, to be my law to govern my church." (D&C 42:58-59.)

It is vital that Church members read and study the four standard works of the Church, for they contain the laws governing the Church and its members.

Many members spend a great deal of time in reading Church books *about* the scriptures but rarely read the scriptures themselves. Our goal is to get the members, and especially the leaders, to read the scriptures.

When we say *read* we don't mean just *read,* but, as Moroni said, "ponder it in your hearts." (Moroni 10:3.) I wondered what the word *ponder* really meant, so I looked it up in the dictionary and found that it means "to weigh in the mind; to meditate or deliberate."

Indeed, there is real value in reading, studying, and pondering the scriptures. It has always been so, but it is especially important today. We should help the leaders and members learn how studying the scriptures can help them to solve their everyday problems. I am grateful for the Prophet Joseph Smith, who as a fourteen-year-old boy found a solution to an everyday problem in the scriptures and who, responding to the admonitions declared in James 1:5-6, went into a grove of trees to pray.

The prophet Nephi recognized in the scriptures the solution of everyday problems as he declared, "I did liken all scriptures unto us, that it might be for our profit and learning." (1 Nephi 19:23.)

Solutions in the Scriptures

The Lord has said, "The Book of Mormon and the holy scriptures are given of me for your instruction; and the power of my Spirit quickeneth all things." (D&C 33:16.)

An abundance of modern revelation is to be found in the Doctrine and Covenants. This scripture explains in detail how to meet today's challenges. For example, think of the tremendous advice given to us in the ninth section, wherein the Lord outlines the technique to use in successful decision-making.

We also have the Pearl of Great Price, which answers many important questions, including "What is the purpose of life?"

We can all relate many experiences in which we have found solutions to our problems in the scriptures.

President Spencer W. Kimball counsels us in this manner: "Let us this year seek to read and understand and apply the principles and inspired counsel found within the [scriptures]. If we do so, we shall discover that our personal *acts* of righteousness *will also bring personal revelation or inspiration* when needed into our own lives." (*Ensign*, September 1975, p. 4.)

Study the Scriptures Regularly

In meeting with priesthood leaders at stake conferences, I frequently ask them to identify some of their weaknesses, and invariably the lack of study of the scriptures is one of the first mentioned.

Let us recognize this problem and encourage stake leaders to study the scriptures every day. It really doesn't matter how long they study—regularity is the main thing. Reading the scriptures can become a most pleasant and profitable way to regularly spend a portion of our time each day. President Kimball has repeatedly asked us to lengthen our stride. This is one area where most of us can profitably lengthen our stride. Many find that studying with their wives and families is interesting and profitable for both.

In one stake, the stake presidency purchased pocket editions of the New Testament for each of the Melchizedek Priesthood leaders and asked them to carry the books in their shirt pockets and read them each day as the opportunity presented itself. They called it the shirt-pocket program. The program was effective. In fact, the stake presidency made me a member of the program by giving me a personalized copy of the New Testament, and I have read many chapters in my spare moments that I probably would not have read otherwise.

Knowledge of the Doctrines Is Needed

I am convinced that a major reason why there are so many inactive persons in the Church is that so many lack a knowledge of the doctrines of the Church. I firmly believe that as we find ways and means to get them together in groups to study the scriptures, and as they pray and attend church, a high percentage of them can be reactivated.

Our sacrament meetings should be an important source of spiritual enlightenment. Members of the Church are really hungering and thirsting for doctrine, but to a considerable extent they are not getting it at our sacrament meetings. On one occasion, in a meeting with a group of bishops, I asked how long it had been since they had had a talk in a sacrament meeting on the subject of faith. One bishop replied that faith was a threadbare subject. Yet to me faith is one of the most important and thrilling gospel subjects to study—and probably the least understood.

President Harold B. Lee stated: "All that we teach in this Church ought to be couched in the scriptures. It ought to be found in the scriptures. We ought to choose our texts from the scriptures. If we want to measure truth, we should measure it by the four standard works, regardless of who writes it. If it is not in the standard works, we may well assume that it is speculation, man's own personal opinion; and if it contradicts what is in the scriptures, it is not true. This is the standard by which we measure all truth." (*Improvement Era,* January 1969, p. 13.)

The Priesthood Program

It may be helpful to call to your attention some matters the Brethren have emphasized for priesthood quorums during the past few years:

1. The responsibility to study the scriptures rests upon the individual priesthood holder. Some have become accustomed to just sitting in a quorum meeting listening rather than actively studying and discussing.

2. We have eliminated the quorum manual in favor of a personal study guide. The purpose of the personal study guide is to encourage and assist the individual priesthood holder in studying the scriptures daily.

3. We have emphasized the leadership role of the quorum president or group leader. That leadership includes discerning the needs of the quorum and determining the subject matter to be discussed or activity to be performed. A quorum president or group leader may assign an instructor to lead a discussion, but it should be the president or the group leader with the help of his counselors who decides what should be discussed.

4. Each priesthood holder, whether or not he is able to at-

tend his quorum or group meetings, should be using the personal study guide to help him in understanding the doctrines and duties outlined in the scriptures. Thus bishopric members, stake presidencies, quorum advisers, and others who cannot regularly attend quorum meetings have the same opportunity for gospel study as do those who attend their quorum and group meetings. In fact, they may have a greater obligation to do so.

5. Studying the scriptures helps an individual to have the Spirit of the Lord. With the example in the scriptures and the influence of the Holy Spirit, personal problems can be solved.

Results of Scripture Study

I bear you my witness that I know that continual study of the scriptures is necessary in order to keep in tune with the Holy Ghost. As our leaders and members make the personal study guide effective in their lives, we will see many changes occur, including:

1. Increased knowledge of the "Plan of Life."
2. More effective service in building the kingdom of God.
3. More love of God and our fellowmen.
4. Increased spirituality among our members.
5. Enlarged testimonies.
6. Greater faith exercised.
7. Greater dedication and willingness to sacrifice.
8. Happier family life with more joy, happiness, growth, and development.

These are only a few of the results that will follow an increased study of the scriptures. Let us emphasize and reemphasize the advisability of the leaders and members forming the habit of daily reading and studying the standard works of the Church as a guide to a rich and rewarding life.

Talents

Developing Our Talents

All of us should be concerned about how to develop our gifts and talents. We should recognize our talents and make up our minds to pay the price necessary to develop them. The price includes, among other things, faith, study, and persistence.

In developing our talents, we must never overlook the fact that we are spirit children of God the Eternal Father, and that He will assist us as we do our part. One way in which He will assist us is opening up opportunities for us to use our talents.

Some do not use their talents because of the fear of men. (See D&C 60:2.) Fear destroys faith and deprives us of many blessings. This is clearly brought out in a revelation in which the Lord said, "Ye endeavored to believe that ye should receive the blessing which was offered unto you; but behold, verily I say unto you there were fears in your hearts, and verily this is the reason that ye did not receive." (D&C 67:3.)

The Spirit of Sharing

As we develop our talents, we should develop the spirit of sharing or giving, not only with those who are closest to us, but with all of God's children. Remember the words of King Benjamin: "When ye are in the service of your fellow beings ye are only in the service of your God." (Mosiah 2:17.) The Lord wants us to enjoy our talents, but He also expects us to use them for the enjoyment and benefit of others and to build the kingdom of God.

The Church is a vehicle for the growth and development of God's children. The priesthood quorums, Young Women, Primary, Sunday School, Relief Society, and other Church organizations in their various activities and programs all contribute to the development of talents and provide opportunities for them to be shared with others.

Challenging leadership opportunities are afforded men, women, and children to become involved in interesting and worthwhile projects. This is not only a great opportunity, but also a responsibility for Latter-day Saints, because the future growth of the Church is dependent upon the development of leaders for general administration as well as missions, stakes, wards, priesthood quorums, and auxiliaries.

Talents may be developed in teaching, speaking, missionary work, music, drama, dancing, athletics, scouting, genealogical and temple work, welfare programs, and compassionate service—all contributing to the development of the Saints.

An Airplane Conversation

Some time ago as I was returning by plane from New York to Salt Lake City, I sat next to a young man, and before long we were engaged in conversation. I asked him where he was from, and he said that he was in the investment business in Minneapolis.

He then asked me where I was from and what my work was, and I told him I was from Salt Lake City and was a Mormon missionary. I asked him what he knew about the Mormon Church, and he said, "Quite a bit." He informed me that he had been an ice-skating instructor at Sun Valley a few years before and had met many Mormons while he was there. He wanted to become better acquainted with the Mormons, so the next summer he secured work in Salt Lake City, where he met many returned missionaries and attended Mormon meetings.

He asked me if I would be interested in knowing what he thought was the most worthwhile thing in the Church. I told him that I would be delighted to have his impression, and he replied that the fact the Church offered every person who was a member an opportunity to serve was the outstanding thing in the Church as far as he could observe.

Our Responsibility

The Church teaches the value and necessity of eternal progression. We progressed in the preexistence, and it is our responsibility and opportunity to develop our talents and progress in this estate and throughout all eternity.

During His earthly ministry, the Savior gave the parable of the entrusted talents, dealing with the requirement that we should develop the talents we are endowed with. (See Matt. 25:14-30.)

In this dispensation He has been equally direct in His charge to His children. He has told us that He has given us many things "for the benefit of the church of the living God, that every man may improve upon his talent, that every man may gain other talents, yea, even an hundred fold." (D&C 82:18.) He has also admonished us that "of him unto whom much is given much is required." (D&C 82:3.)

Clearly, our obligation is to use and develop the gifts and talents we have been blessed with, and human experience confirms the soundness of this doctrine.

Feelings of Inadequacy

Sometimes when a person is asked to accept a position in the Church, he will say, "Oh, I can't do that. I haven't as much experience or education as someone else that may have been serving." But if we have faith, and if we will study, work, and pray, the Lord will make it possible for us to accomplish things that seem impossible.

Our measuring stick should not be someone else's accomplishments, but our own capabilities. Are we truly doing our best? Are we anxious to develop our talents to the greatest degree and use them in building the kingdom of God? When we do this, we develop our talents, we are happy, and we grow in knowledge and spirit.

Recognize Your Talents

A few years ago, President Kimball and I attended a branch Sunday School in Cuzco, Peru. A young missionary from North America played the piano for the meeting. Afterwards, President Kimball asked if any of the local members could play the piano. The branch president replied that one of his counselors could play two hymns. President Kimball then asked that the man play the two hymns for sacrament meeting, and he did so. After the meeting, President Kimball suggested that the counselor continue to develop his musical talent and play the piano for all Church services. Probably this man had never recognized that he had a talent that could be developed by Church service.

Magnify Each Talent

Recently a new convert told how he had three Church assignments: putting the flag up each day in front of the chapel, passing out the hymnbooks for each meeting, and being a home teacher. This man was rendering service, was happy, and was preparing himself for other assignments.

Sometimes we hear reports that someone thinks his or her assignment isn't very important. This reminds me of the young man who gave his intended wife a diamond engagement ring and remarked, "It isn't very big." She replied, "It's as big as we make it." So it is with every call to serve in building the kingdom of God. It's as big as we make it. There are no unimportant callings in the Church.

As we develop the spirit of sharing our talents, we will find peace, happiness, joy, and contentment as well as growth and development. Yes, we will be magnified, and our talents will be increased, "yea, even an hundred fold." (D&C 82:18.)

Temples

The Temple Ordinances

If one desires to enjoy eternal life, he must learn the laws of heaven and obey them, and the temple is the place where much of this knowledge can be obtained. President Brigham Young had this to say regarding the endowment: "Your endowment is, to receive all those ordinances in the house of the Lord, which are necessary for you, after you have departed this life, to enable you to walk back to the presence of the Father, passing the angels who stand as sentinels, being enabled to give them the key words, the signs and tokens, pertaining to the holy Priesthood, and gain eternal exaltation in spite of earth and hell." (*Discourses of Brigham Young* [Deseret Book, 1966], p. 416.)

The temple endowment, however, is a separate ordinance from the sealing ordinances. The endowment is an ordinance for the individual, but sealing ordinances pertain to the family relationship. The sealing ordinance is the highest ordinance that one can receive in the temple. It is by this ordinance that one receives the blessings of eternal family units.

We are charged with the responsibility of taking the gospel to every nation, kindred, tongue, and people. Those who do not have the opportunity to hear the gospel in the flesh will have it in the spirit. In other words, the gospel will be preached to them in the spirit world. (See 1 Pet. 3:18-20; 4:6.)

The gospel provides that all who accept its principles shall repent and be baptized by immersion in water, to be followed by spirit baptism, or the giving and receiving of the Holy Ghost.

Grandfather's Interest in Temple Work

Grandfather Richards began temple work early for his dead ancestors. In his journal, under date of November 23, 1895, he notes that he had had baptisms by proxy performed for 2,801 members of the Richards family and those who had intermarried with them, and that the baptisms had been properly recorded in his family record book. He had also had baptisms performed for over fourteen hundred members of the Dewey family, for over four hundred of the Comstock family, and for many of the Snyder family. The last fifteen years of his life saw these numbers greatly increased, for his interest in the work grew as he advanced in years. (Franklin L. West, *Life of Franklin D. Richards* [Salt Lake City: Deseret News Press, 1924], p. 242.)

With the completion of four temples in Utah, the demand for genealogical information became so great that Grandfather invited a number of prominent members of the Church to meet in his office to consider ways and means to assist the people in obtaining their genealogies. At this meeting on November 13, 1894, the Utah Genealogical Society was organized, its purpose being purely benevolent, namely, to collect, compile, establish, and maintain a genealogical library for the use of its members, and also to be educational in disseminating information regarding all such matters.

On December 28, 1897, the Utah State Historical Society was founded, with its membership comprising representative Mormon and non-Mormon citizens. Grandfather Richards was the first president and remained in that position until his death.

Grandfather was a member of the building committee of the Logan Temple, and he participated in the dedication of the St. George, Manti, Logan, and Salt Lake temples.

Manifestation in Manti

Speaking of the dedication of the Manti Temple, May 21, 1888, Grandfather Richards said, "When we dedicated the Temple at Manti, many of the brethren and sisters saw the presence of spiritual beings, discernible only by the inward eye. The prophets Joseph, Hyrum, Brigham and various other Apostles that have gone, were seen, and not only this, but the ears of many of the faithful were touched, and they heard the music of the heavenly choir." (Ibid., p. 242.)

The spirit of temple work is beautifully set forth in the following excerpts of a discourse delivered by him in the Logan Tabernacle, the day after the dedication of the temple at that place:

"The temples, the houses of our God, when acceptably dedicated, become to us the gates of Heaven. They are esteemed most holy unto the Lord of all places upon the earth; therein the faithful approach nearest unto God and obtain the greatest fellowship and inspiration of the Holy Spirit. While in the Temple with the chief authorities of the Church, the impression was irresistible that the fellowship of the heavens was near us, that our Savior was near us, and his Spirit was abundantly manifested in the midst of the congregation. We felt that our ancient father, Adam, Noah and Abraham, who, the revelations inform us, have entered into their exaltation and sit upon their thrones, were all earnestly interested in our offering.

"When we go to the Temple, let us go to meet the Lord, forget the cares of the world, and feel as Jacob did when he slept on the stones and said that it was none other than the gate of heaven. In these sacred places you feel as though the spirits of the dead are around you, guarding, directing and aiding you. Then you will begin to think of holy things, and when you return to your homes the good feelings of the Temple will go with you to your firesides and neighbors, and the fragrance of heaven will come to be shed abroad, and others will want to go there that they may be like unto you, and enjoy similar blessings. And you will dream and hear the voice of the dead, and the sweet whisperings of the Holy Spirit will tell you what to do. And the heavens and the earth will be bound together. Death will lose its terrors. You will find that you have more relatives in heaven than on earth, and in old age you will want to pass away, that you may rejoice in their companionship." (Ibid., pp. 242-43.)

Salvation Is Universally Available

The ministry of Christ was not confined to the few who lived on the earth in the meridian of time or at the present time; the plan of salvation is for those who have lived in all ages of the world. The vicarious effect of the atonement of Jesus Christ brought about the redemption of all mankind from mortal death and provided the means whereby personal sins could be forgiven.

The essential ordinances of the gospel must be performed by the living for themselves and vicariously for the dead. However, the doctrine of vicarious service for the dead by the living does not affect the right of the dead to accept or reject such service.

Why a Temple?

For the living, such ordinances as ordination to the priesthood, baptism, and the bestowal of the Holy Ghost may be performed in any proper place, but through modern revelation we are told that certain ordinances, such as the endowment, eternal marriage, and other sealing ordinances for both the living and the dead, and baptism for the dead, must be performed in a temple.

The temple endowment helps to clarify the object of man's existence. It provides, in effect, a course of instruction wherein

many of the answers are given to the questions: What is the
purpose of life? Where did we come from? Why are we here?
Where do we go after this life?

It is important to realize that the blessings of the temple are
not limited to any special class; they are available to all worthy
members, properly accredited.

A temple is also a retreat from the vicissitudes of life. It is a
place of prayer—a place where the divine spark in man or the
infinite in man can seek the infinite in God.

The Lord has provided that we can be exalted in His kingdom by obedience to the laws and ordinances of the gospel,
many of which will be administered to God's children in the
house of the Lord.

Testimony

A Word with Special Meaning

In The Church of Jesus Christ of Latter-day Saints, members frequently use words that have a special meaning to them, one of which is *testimony*.

Members bear or relate their testimonies to other members at special testimony meetings and at times avail themselves of the opportunity to bear testimonies to nonmembers.

In bearing their testimonies, members generally testify that they know that God lives; that His Son, Jesus Christ, is our Savior and Redeemer; and that the restored gospel of Jesus Christ is the divine plan of life that brings happiness and growth to those who accept it and make it a part of their daily lives.

President Harold B. Lee expressed it this way: "Within the Gospel of Jesus Christ may be found the solution of every problem confronting us, which will enable us to find happiness here and eternal life in the world to come." (*Church News*, March 9, 1974, p. 2.)

It has been said that the purpose of the gospel is to change people's lives—to make bad people good and good people better, to change human nature; and how true this is!

President Brigham Young said, "You cannot find a compass on the earth, that points so directly, as the Gospel Plan of Salvation. It has a place for everything and puts everything in its place." (*Journal of Discourses* 3:96.)

Some members of the Church possess powerful and unfaltering testimonies, while others possess less forceful testimonies. It should be recognized that testimonies can be acquired, testimonies can be kept, and testimonies can be lost. It is not uncommon to hear Church members declare that their testimony is their most prized possession.

A convert from Seattle, in answer to the question "What has the Church done for you?" replied, "Everything—my life now has purpose and meaning. Now, what can I do for the Lord? I owe him my all."

Another convert living in Arizona had this to say: "One brother was extremely instrumental in our becoming members of the Church. We will ever be indebted to him and thankful to him for asking us what we knew about the Mormon Church and if we would like to know more. Through the missionary discussions we were thoroughly convinced that this was the true Church. And the thing that has changed my life the most is that I have found a purpose in life and a certain peace of mind I have never felt before. I know with all my heart that this is the true Church and that Christ lives and God lives."

These converts' testimonies are inspiring and emphasize the value of the gospel to them and to their families.

How to Gain a Testimony

I have borne my testimony many times to people who were interested in knowing more about the Church, and they have asked, "How can I obtain a conviction of the truthfulness of the restored gospel?—yes, a testimony to this effect." My answer has been to study the gospel, pray, and attend church.

This formula, when followed, will bring a conviction or testimony that the restored gospel of Jesus Christ is true, and that when one accepts the gospel plan and lives its principles, it will bring them peace, happiness, growth, and development. However, to obtain a testimony, one must have a real desire to know the truth and must be willing to exert considerable effort.

Step 1. Study the Gospel

The Lord has told us that "the glory of God is intelligence." (D&C 93:36.) In the standard works, we are given the information that we need to adjust our lives and prepare ourselves so that no matter what may transpire, we will be prepared. Study of the scriptures assists us in spiritual achievement.

The interested person must study the gospel, and the gospel is to be found primarily in the four standard works of the Church.

Jesus said, "Ye shall know the truth, and the truth shall make you free." (John 8:32.) I feel sure that part of this freedom must be freedom from ignorance. Through study of the scriptures, we can understand our relationship to God and how the basic gospel principles apply to our daily lives. Our study should be constant and intensive, as the gospel of Jesus Christ embraces all truth.

Step 2. Pray

The second step to acquire a testimony is to pray.

The Prophet Joseph Smith observed that "it is the first principle of the gospel to know for a certainty the character of God, and to know that we may converse with Him as one man converses with another." (History of the Church 6:305.)

Near the end of the Book of Mormon, Moroni, a great leader, gave this promise: "And when ye shall receive these things, I would exhort you that ye would ask God, the Eternal Father, in the name of Christ, if these things are not true; and if ye shall ask with a sincere heart, with real intent, having faith in Christ, he will manifest the truth of it unto you, by the power of the Holy Ghost. And by the power of the Holy Ghost ye may know the truth of all things." (Moro. 10:4-5.)

Although this promise specifically refers to the Book of Mormon, I am sure that as you study the Bible, Doctrine and Covenants, and Pearl of Great Price, you will find that the promise is likewise applicable to these scriptures.

Prayer plays a vital part in our religious thinking and in our daily lives. One of my convert friends told me, "Because the elders emphasized that we should pray, I did. I had barely asked the questions when the beautiful answer came. Yes, that was the start of my new life."

Another convert said, "I used to pray—not often—but I did pray before we became members. I prayed that someday my husband and I would grow closer together. I never thought it would be, but the Church was my answer. We found the power of prayer. I'm so thankful for the Church."

Prayer, then, must accompany study, in order for one to obtain a testimony of the truthfulness of the restored gospel.

Step 3. Attend Church

The third part of the formula to obtain a testimony is to attend church and become involved in church activities.

My Arizona convert friend also had this to say: "The first time we visited a ward meeting, I felt such a warm, loving feeling. All the people seemed to have smiles on their faces and hearty handshakes for us. We felt so welcome, and we knew we wanted to be a part of all this. This was the only way." She continued, "Another aspect of the Church I love is its constant learning, developing, and growing power. I'm grateful for the opportunity to work in the Church, because this constant contact is helping us to grow and develop in the gospel."

Another convert expressed it this way: "As my husband and I were baptized, I had no idea just how involved we would become. My first calling was that of chorister in sacrament meeting. Then I was asked to be a Mia Maid leader. I asked the question, 'What is a Mia Maid?' I learned from experience that it's a girl, the delightful age of fourteen. The girls have so much enthusiasm and energy. I am so thrilled with my calling in MIA. It keeps me feeling young and needed and busy. My husband, too, has held many positions in the ward, and his determination and dedication have been a strength to me."

How to Keep Your Testimony

To those who feel that they have a firm testimony, remember that a testimony is never static. A testimony can be lost. To remain alive, it must be fed. Continue to study, pray, attend church, and be involved. This will not only keep your testimony alive, but it will also expand and become more meaningful in your life.

I bear my testimony that the Holy Ghost has borne witness to me that God lives and is the Father of our spirits, that Jesus Christ is our Redeemer and Savior, and that Joseph Smith was a great prophet chosen by God to restore the gospel in its fulness and the power to act in his name in this dispensation.

The Holy Ghost has also borne witness to me that President Spencer W. Kimball is a modern-day prophet who leads and directs The Church of Jesus Christ of Latter-day Saints today. May the Lord bless and sustain him in this calling, and may we sustain him and have the courage to follow his counsel.

This testimony has a beneficial influence in every phase of my life, and I can readily understand why so many Church members continually bear witness that their testimony is their most prized possession.

Thanksgiving

A History to Be Thankful For

With so many days and weeks in the year devoted to commercial causes and purposes, it is good to have a period set aside for giving thanks. Thanksgiving is the time for enjoying family get-togethers and the ritual of the feast. It is a time for counting our blessings and good fortune.

We give thanks that our forefathers patterned communities to serve the spiritual and material needs of the people. Likewise, we give thanks that ours is a land where we can still laugh and dream and hope and speak our minds and worship as we please.

Yes, we have much to be thankful for. To the Pilgrims who first instituted Thanksgiving in America, there was real meaning in the celebration they held. They had passed through a severe winter. A number of those who made the voyage in the *Mayflower* had died. All had been hungry and cold. The bitterness of the winter was followed by a trying summer. Every effort was made to produce food to avoid suffering in the next winter. They labored hard and they prayed. Their very existence was at stake. As harvest time came and there seemed to be sufficient to meet their needs, they sensed deep feelings of gratitude to God. How could they resist expressing their thanks?

It was this excellence and purity that God recognized in our Pilgrim ancestors who came to America for the love of truth and to worship God according to the dictates of their conscience. It was this excellence that preserved them and established them in the new country. As long as they maintained this excellence and purity, they prospered.

They were powerful in that they had faith to receive inspiration from God. Later, under this inspiration, they joined with other inspired men to draw up and establish the greatest constitution that has ever been known. Our forefathers purchased with their own blood the power to draw up and frame this great instrument. They were men who went into the Revolutionary War, pledging their lives, their fortunes, and their sacred honor; and they placed everything they possessed upon the altar of liberty.

Pioneers like Pilgrims

When the Utah pioneers held their first Thanksgiving after their first full year in the Salt Lake Valley, they did so under much the same circumstances as the Pilgrims. They too had had their trying winter; they too had known hunger and cold and had labored and prayed for a bounteous harvest. To express the thanksgiving that they felt in their hearts was but to acknowledge the hand of God in rewarding them for their efforts.

More than a century of harvests bears eloquent record to the rightness of their thanksgiving and the correctness of Brigham Young's historic words: "This is the place."

No People So Blessed

As we celebrate Thanksgiving Day, let us catch the spirit that underlies the meaning of this day. Let us be grateful. No people in all the world are as blessed as we are. As we experience this feeling of gratitude, let us direct our thanks to God. All that we have comes from him. Our blessings are not due to our efforts alone. Let us be grateful that He gave us life and that we have faith to believe in Him.

Let us review the blessings we enjoy as citizens of this great land. We are free; no iron hand determines what we shall do, and no iron curtain hems us in. We may come and go as we please. America is God's gift to us; our nation was established by Him so that freedom might be ours. And with this freedom, we enjoy so many of the bounties of life. We seem to be blessed with an oversupply of food, clothing, housing, cars, and, in fact, nearly all consumer goods.

In many other parts of the world, large numbers of people are poorly fed, clothed, and housed. We as a nation have made many major contributions to the welfare of the needy peoples of the world. Thank the Lord for this. We can be thankful that we are a nation of homeowners. Let us truly appreciate our families and understand the real value of our home life as a means of developing a strong nation. Let us be truly thankful to our forebears, who made great sacrifices that we might enjoy the comforts of today. Let us appreciate that no one is self-sufficient, but that life is a cooperative affair. The more we count our blessings, the more we realize that they all come from God.

Our Spiritual Heritage

As we consider our blessings, we come to realize that the material blessings are really the least of what we have. But so many of us allow the material to obscure the spiritual. Above all else, let us fully appreciate the spiritual heritage that we enjoy. And spirituality is an attitude, an atmosphere of living. Spirituality comes from surrendering to the eternally great things and permitting them to dominate our lives.

The sin of ingratitude is not only a failure to express thanks, but it is also an accumulation of many other sins that have made us selfish and grasping. Only the selfish are ungrateful.

Yes, gratitude is one of the traits of genuine character. Persons with great character are usually devoted to the principle of gratitude and receive real happiness from this. In the final analysis, gratitude must be expressed in heartfelt service, both to our fellowmen and to God. Those who have time and money have every right to spend them as they will. However, in sharing, new courage is brought to someone struggling, a dawn of new hope to someone weary and fainthearted, a new chance and new inspiration to someone to pull him through a crisis.

The Satisfaction of Sharing

Wealth and time are but human privileges committed to one whereby he may serve his fellowmen and thus receive joy. Yes, satisfaction comes from sharing ourselves, our affection, our energy, our time, and our earthly possessions. A wise man once said, "He who receives a benefit should never forget it; he who bestows it should never remember it."

The final test of men is not what they have, but what they do with what they have. An inscription on an old English grave reads:

> *What I gave I have,*
> *What I spent I had,*
> *What I left I lost,*
> *By not giving it.*

The Lord commanded us to be grateful and thankful in all things. We cannot be truly thankful and have the correct perspective on life if we leave God out of our thinking and planning. We are told that the earth is the Lord's and the fulness thereof, but He has given it to us for our enjoyment and welfare.

Izaak Walton interestingly stated, "God has two dwellings—one in heaven and the other in a meek and thankful heart." At Thanksgiving time, let us pause to reflect, take stock of ourselves, and be thankful and grateful. May we thank the Lord by doing His will in serving our fellowmen. For as the Savior taught, "Inasmuch as ye have done it unto one of the least of these my brethren, ye have done it unto me." (Matt. 25:40.)

Tithing

Our Share in Philanthropy

Our business should be to build the kingdom of God. Many of us have said, in our more generous and unselfish moments, "If I only had the wealth, I would build a beautiful church, provide a school for underprivileged children, supply a hospital where it is needed," and so forth.

Probably few of us will have the great wealth needed to do any of these things by ourselves; nevertheless, each of us, as we have the desire, can have a share in such wonderful projects by our contributions, including the payment of our tithes and offerings.

Throughout the ages, the Lord has commanded His people to remember the needy and to pay tithes and offerings for the purpose of building the kingdom. In this dispensation, He has revealed that this is "a day of sacrifice, and a day for the tithing of my people." (D&C 64:23.)

Those Who Rob God

A substantial number of the Saints are today honestly meeting this requirement to pay tithes and offerings. Yet many are negligent in observing this commandment.

The Lord has said: "Will a man rob God? Yet ye have robbed me. But ye say, Wherein have we robbed thee? In tithes and offerings. . . . Bring ye all the tithes into the storehouse, . . . and prove me now herewith, saith the Lord of hosts, if I will not open you the windows of heaven, and pour you out a blessing, that there shall not be room enough to receive it." (Mal. 3:8, 10.)

When men, women, and children are honest with God and pay their tithes and offerings, the Lord gives them wisdom whereby they can do with the remainder as much as or more than they could if they had not been honest with the Lord.

Learning to Pay Tithing

When I was a very young boy my parents taught me about tithing. They told me that it was a commandment of our Father in heaven and a good way for us to show our love for Him and our appreciation for all the blessings He gives to us. They taught me that tithing was to give to the Lord one penny out of every dime, or one dime out of every dollar I earned.

Although I started selling eggs when I was a young boy, I felt pretty grown up. I had my own money to spend. Some was used to start a savings account, and always I set my tithing aside.

I also earned money doing errands and odd jobs for people in the neighborhood, and Father paid me for helping on the ranch in the summer. So by the end of the year I earned a lot of money (at least it seemed like a lot to me), and I was very proud to take my tithing, in a big envelope filled with nickels and dimes and small bills, to the bishop at tithing settlement time.

I still have a tithing receipt (it was then called a Bishop's Storehouse Receipt) that was given to me when I was eight years old. It was for $7.50, and it is dated December 31, 1908. It is among my prized possessions.

I am grateful that I had a father and a mother who taught me as a very young boy the joy of work and the importance of spending less than I made so that I could have something saved for a "rainy day." I am grateful, too, that I learned as a boy the importance of paying my tithing, as I am sure that many of the blessings I have enjoyed throughout my life have come to me because I have been obedient to the law of tithing.

The younger boys and girls are when they learn these important lessons, the more these principles will become a part of their lives and help them to become successful, happy people.

Remember the words of the Lord Jesus, that "It is more blessed to give than to receive." (Acts 20:35.) What are riches for, then? To be used in doing good! Therefore, let us dedicate our means to building the kingdom of God. Let us this day resolve to be honest with the Lord in the payment of our tithes and offerings.

Tithes are sacred funds, and the Lord in this dispensation has revealed that it "shall be disposed of by a council, composed of the First Presidency of my Church, and of the bishop and his council, . . . and by mine own voice unto them." (D&C 120:1.)

Needs of the Expanding Church

With the accelerated growth of the Church throughout the world, more and more buildings and facilities are required—chapels, schools, seminaries, temples, mission homes, visitor centers, and many other buildings. Not only does the construction of these new facilities require the expenditure of large sums of capital, but the operation and maintenance of these buildings entail heavy financial responsibilities.

The Church is designed to take care of the spiritual and temporal needs of its members, both living and dead; and the pattern encompasses such programs as education, missionary, welfare, auxiliary, and social services and genealogy. These programs, functioning on a worldwide basis, require great financial assistance.

We have been looking to this day for more than a hundred years, and as we keep the commandments of the Lord, I know

He will open up the way whereby we can meet the financial obligations relative to the growth and development of the
Church, as well as our own responsibilities.

Repent of Worshipping Property

As we consider ourselves trustees of wealth for the benefit of
God's children, we should not worship property, whether it be
of great or small value. If we are guilty of worshipping property,
then we have need to repent and straighten out our values. A
person who places the wealth of this world in the scales against
the things of God evidences little understanding of eternal values. We talk of making sacrifices to build the kingdom of God,
but the word to me is a misnomer. To be able to participate in
the building of the kingdom is a great privilege and opens the
way to many blessings.

A Christmas Gift to the Chapel

Recently I dedicated a beautiful little chapel, and at that
time I was told that in order to pay the balance of the ward's
share of the construction cost, the bishop asked all members to
limit Christmas presents to small children and to donate the
amount thus saved to the building fund. The members responded beautifully, considering this an opportunity to receive
a blessing rather than a sacrifice; and at the dedicatory service,
many bore witness to this effect.

As long as one is honest with the Lord, the amount paid is
not material. The widow's or child's mite is as important and
acceptable as the rich man's offerings.

Wealth

The Gospel of Work

God has given us our free agency, but we are required to work for our sustenance, growth, and development. We frequently refer to the gospel as the gospel of work.

This principle incorporates the necessity of sustaining ourselves and our families. To properly fulfill this requirement in this day, we must be financially responsible and strong. Being strong financially does not necessarily mean being wealthy with earthly possessions; it means possessing sufficient to meet our requirements and living within our income rather than overextending.

Stay Out of Debt

In modern revelation the Lord has given us these commandments: "Behold, it is said in my laws, or forbidden, to get in debt to thine enemies." (D&C 64:27.) "And again, verily I say unto you, concerning your debts—behold it is my will that you shall pay all your debts." (D&C 104:78.)

We are told that President Brigham Young repeatedly counseled the Saints to get out of debt and stay out of debt. Other Latter-day prophets have given similar counsel. President Joseph F. Smith is reported to have counseled the Saints to "get out of debt and keep out of debt, and then you will be financially as well as spiritually free."

President Heber J. Grant said in one of his sermons, "If there is any one thing that will bring peace and contentment into the human heart, and into the family, it is to live within our means; and if there is one thing that is grinding and discouraging and disheartening, it is to have debts and obligations that one cannot meet." (*Relief Society Magazine* 19:302.)

Today much unhappiness results from financial problems; they are a major factor in unhappy marriages, many of which result in divorce.

Avoid the Unwise Use of Credit

Personal financial weaknesses come about primarily through unwise use of credit and obligating ourselves for more than we receive. This frequently brings about bankruptcy; and unfortunately, bankruptcies have greatly increased during the past few years. I counsel you to get out of debt and stay out of debt; if it is necessary to use credit, use it wisely and sparingly.

Financial strength is realized by keeping God's commandments, one of which is the payment of an honest tithe, and by developing habits of work, thrift, and living within one's income. It is vital to our welfare and happiness that we be strong financially as well as spiritually, morally, mentally, and physically.

Our Resources Are the Lord's Blessings

Regardless of the difficulties existing in the world today, we, as a people, must recognize that we have been blessed abundantly with the resources of this world; yet we know that whatever we have is the Lord's, and that He has blessed us with these things to see how we will use them. I think it might be said that life is God's greatest gift to man, and what we do with our life is our gift to God.

President Brigham Young, in referring to making our life a

gift to God, said: "Our religion is worth everything to us, and for it we should be willing to employ our time, our talent, our means, our energies, our lives." (*Journal of Discourses* 11:119.) "If we do right, there will be an eternal increase among this people in talent, strength of intellect, and earthly wealth, from this time henceforth, and forever." (*JD* 1:110.)

The Temptations of Wealth

It is interesting to note that promises of earthly wealth and increased talents are made to those who live the gospel principles, and counsel is given to use our talents and wealth for the building of the kingdom. Many scriptures, however, contain words of admonition regarding temptations brought about through the acquisition of wealth and its use for unrighteous purposes.

The Apostle Paul, in writing to his beloved associate Tmothy, told him that "the love of money is the root of all evil," and to "charge them that are rich in this world, that they be not highminded, nor trust in uncertain riches, but in the living God, who giveth us richly all things to enjoy: That they do good, that they be rich in good works, ready to distribute." (1 Tim. 6:17-18.)

Follow Counsel and Prosper

Throughout the history of the Church, our leaders have taught the value of the principles of work, industry, and thrift; and as these principles have been practiced, Church members have prospered in numerous ways. Likewise, members have been counseled to establish and maintain their economic independence, and employment-creating industries have been encouraged.

In furtherance of these teachings, every man who has property and means should live so as to obtain wisdom to know how to use them in the best possible way to produce the greatest amount of good for himself, for his family, for his fellowmen, and for the kingdom of God.

Attitude toward Possessions

Again quoting President Young: "When this people are prepared to properly use the riches of this world for the building up of the kingdom of God, He is ready and willing to bestow them upon us. . . . I like to see men get rich by their industry, prudence, management and economy, and then devote it to the building up of the kingdom of God upon the earth." (*JD* 11:114-15.)

Andrew Carnegie, one of this country's great philanthropists, is said to have stated his attitude toward wealth as follows: "This, then, is held to be the duty of the man of wealth: First to set an example of modesty, unostentatious living, shunning display or extravagance; to provide moderately for the legitimate wants of those dependent upon him; and after doing so, to consider all surplus revenues which come to him simply as trust funds, which he is called upon to administer, and strictly bound as a matter of duty to administer in the manner in which, in his judgment, is best calculated to produce the most beneficial results for the community—the man of wealth thus becoming the mere trustee and agent for his poorer brethren, bringing to their service his superior wisdom, experience and ability to administer, doing for them better than they would or could do for themselves."

With this philosophy of wealth in mind, one might properly say: "What I am worth is what I am doing for other people." In many respects, the real test of man is his attitude toward his earthly possessions.

The True Riches of Testimony

I know that God lives and that Jesus is the Christ, our Savior and Redeemer, and this knowledge is far more important than earthly riches. And I know that the gospel in its fulness has has been restored in this dispensation through the instrumentality of the Prophet Joseph Smith and that there is a living prophet at the head of the Church today. This is likewise of more value than any amount of earthly wealth.

However, a testimony alone will not save us. It is keeping the commandments of God—living the life of a true Latter-day Saint. It is important, then, to appreciate that the gospel has to be lived in order to be fully realized and its power received.

Therefore, let us dispense with the means that the Lord has given us to enrich the lives of others who are less fortunate than we are and to build the kingdom of God, that we may make of our lives a good gift to God.

Work

A Marvelous Philosophy

President David O. McKay said, "Let us realize that the privilege to work is a gift, that the power to work is a blessing, that love of work is success."

What a marvelous philosophy—the gospel of work! Yet today, as in earlier times, many misguided individuals embrace the philosophy of idleness, feeling that the world owes them a living. Many have a desire to destroy the establishment that has been built upon productive effort.

In this dispensation the Lord has many times confirmed the eternal principle of work. We have been told that there is no place in the Church for the idler "except he repent and mend his ways" (D&C 75:29), and "he that is idle shall not eat the bread nor wear the garments of the laborer" (D&C 42:42).

Ever since its organization, the Church has encouraged its members to establish and maintain their economic independence; it has encouraged thrift and fostered the establishment of employment-creating industries.

At the time the present welfare program of the Church was established, President Heber J. Grant explained that the primary purpose was "to set up . . . a system under which the curse of idleness would be done away with, the evils of a dole abolished, and independence, industry, thrift and self respect be once more established amongst our people. The aim of the Church is to help the people to help themselves. Work is to be re-enthroned as the ruling principle of the lives of our Church membership." (*Conference Report,* October 1936, p. 3.)

I encourage all to accept wholeheartedly the principle of effective work and make it a vital part of our lives.

The Desire for Excellence Is Godly

The desire for superior achievement comes from our Father in heaven. However, too many people are imbued with the spirit of "just getting by." This spirit comes from the evil one. Let us avoid the habit of "just getting by," as it will rob us of the choicest rewards.

Whether our work is mainly mental or physical or is a combination of both, we should learn to do it well, cultivate the proper attitude, and develop work habits that will produce superior results. These habits will become a part of us.

To develop a love of work, I suggest two guidelines: (1) Set worthwhile objectives. (2) Be satisfied only with superior achievement. Let us consider that each day is a success when we accomplish a worthwhile objective, and any day is a failure if it passes without some worthwhile achievement.

Our Long-Term Goal

Proper appreciation of life's purpose is a great help in developing worthwhile objectives. The restored gospel of Jesus Christ answers the questions "Where did we come from?" "Why are we here?" "Where do we go after this life?" With this knowledge, we are in a preferred position to set worthwhile objectives and goals, both short-range and long-range.

We need not hesitate to establish our long-term objective as exaltation in the celestial kingdom, or eternal life. Each of us is entitled to immortality through the atoning sacrifice of Jesus Christ, our Savior and Redeemer, but in order to enjoy eternal life, or exaltation in the celestial kingdom, we must *work* out our own salvation day by day.

Objectives and goals should be not only worthwhile, but also realistic. They should be an incentive to work effectively. Thus the setting of realistic objectives and achieving them becomes an important part of the process of eternal progression.

The Savior often emphasized the doctrine of unselfishness and sacrifice, and it is apparent that there is no real success or happiness in being self-centered and selfish. Let me suggest, therefore, the advisability of engaging in some work that involves service to our fellowmen and some sacrifice of our time, talents, and means. It is through this type of work that one can easily develop a love for, as well as a love of, people.

Learn to "Be There"

The Church furnishes many opportunities for work and service, regardless of age.

One of the happiest persons I have seen recently was an eighty-six-year-old woman who was busily engaged in doing temple work in the Salt Lake Temple. It was evident that she loved her work. To her, work itself, with a sense of accomplishment, was the way to avoid getting old.

I will be eternally grateful to the president of the stake I was raised in as a young man. His motto was "Be there," and it meant to work effectively, to magnify one's calling. Learning this lesson as a young man has had a great effect in my life.

The philosophy of work and the extra mile is a sound philosophy. It is a vital part of the gospel of Jesus Christ which will lead us to eternal life. I encourage all to accept wholeheartedly the principle of effective work and make it a vital part of our lives, as the pioneers did in their lives.

This is brought out in an interesting letter received from a sister missionary, who stated:

"'With hard work, deep humility and sincere prayer, you

will succeed.' As I read this sentence on my first day in the mission field, I thought: I want to be a successful missionary.

"I found that to me hard work meant going the 'extra mile' in doing more than is required. One experience I shall never forget is the day my companion and I found three really golden families because we asked the golden questions twenty times instead of fifteen. If we had not asked more than the required fifteen, we would not have been blessed in finding them, because they were the sixteenth, eighteenth, and nineteenth families that we asked. My companion and I were given the blessings of teaching two of these families. Satan was really working hard on these choice families, and then I learned again the importance of sincere prayer. Sincere prayer, fasting, and our testimonies of the true gospel were really the only weapons we had to fight Satan. But the Lord does answer our prayers.

"I was truly humbled as my companion and I watched these lovely people baptized by the true authority. Tears of happiness came into my eyes as I realized the blessings that the Lord had given to those coming into the Church and to my companion and me through hard work."

Paying the Price

Superior achievement comes when one makes up his mind to be successful and is willing to pay the price, or magnify his calling. This involves developing faith in the Lord Jesus Christ and faith in ourselves, always remembering that we are spirit children of God. It involves study and training, coupled with planning, discipline, and work—yes, going the extra mile.

Teach children the importance of work and assist them in preparing for superior achievements. Don't deprive them of the blessings that come from proper work habits. Eleanor Roosevelt once remarked that "the surest way to make it hard for children is to make it easy for them."

My Parents—and Fifty Chickens

We may not realize it, but when we are very young we set the patterns that follow us all through our lives. It is important that we set good patterns.

My father and mother believed firmly in the principle of work, and they saw to it that their six boys had plenty of work to do. Although I was the youngest in the family, I had my share of jobs around the house and yard. To make sure I wouldn't run out of a job and to develop in me a sense of responsibility, Father had some chicken coops and runs built in our backyard. These he filled with a flock of about fifty chickens. It was my responsibility to feed and water the chickens, keep the coops clean, and gather the eggs.

In the summer I gathered lawn clippings and put them to dry on the roof of the chicken coop. When they were dry, I put them in bags. In the winter, I put the clippings in pans, poured hot water over them, and fed them to the chickens for green food.

By giving the chickens good care, we had more than enough eggs to supply the needs of our family. Father told me that I could have the extra eggs to sell and use the money for my own needs. I found the neighbors were very glad to have fresh eggs. I soon established an egg route and had regular customers. My customers became my good friends, and this was the beginning of many happy associations that lasted for many years. I am grateful that I had a father and mother who taught me as a very young boy the joy of working, the value of spending less than I made, and the importance of paying my tithing.

The Importance of Loyalty

Another essential factor to consider in a discussion of work is loyalty. Loyalty to an employer or a cause one is working for is a key step in developing a love of work.

Teach children to recognize their obligations. Teach them to be loyal to their families, to their employers, to the Church, to their country, and to any worthy cause they espouse.

How can you find time to teach these things to your children and what is the best way to do it, you ask? You will find the time and a most effective way as you hold your weekly family home evening, as you have been counseled to do.

Learn to Relax

In searching for ways to develop a love of work, we must not overlook the matter of relaxation. Although work is absolutely essential to achievement, relaxation and proper rest are likewise necessary. The power to pace one's self is an important factor in developing a love of work. The Lord expects each of us to work out a proper balance between work and relaxation as well as the physical and spiritual aspects of life.

It will be to our eternal advantage to recognize that work is the secret of growth, progress, and happiness both temporally and spiritually. Set worthwhile and realistic objectives, and be satisfied only with superior achievement. Accept every opportunity to serve in building the kingdom of God. I bear witness that as we do our part, the Lord will make us equal to every task that we are called upon to perform.

Sources

Adversity

"The First and Second Estates," general conference address, October 3, 1965.

"Life's Problems—Our Opportunities," Brigham Young University, April 7, 1970.

"The Purpose of Life: To Be Proved," general conference address, October 1, 1971.

Church Expansion

"A New Era of Growth and Development," twelve-stake fireside, Brigham Young University, September 25, 1977.

Devotional address, LDS Institute of Religion, University of Utah, October 21, 1977.

Decisions

"Choose the Right," Brigham Young University, November 3, 1964.

"Choose the Right," address to Latter-day Saints Student Association, University of Utah, November 17, 1972.

Eternal Progression

"Be Humble and Strong," general conference address, October 1, 1966.

"Eternal Values in a World of Change," Brigham Young University, June 7, 1967.

"Genealogy: A Priesthood Responsibility," genealogical seminar, Brigham Young University, June 22, 1967.

"The Spirit of Man," baccalaureate address, Benemerito de las Americas, Mexico City, August 22, 1968.

Faith and Works

"Building Leaders," Brigham Young University, March 16, 1976.

"Eternal Values in a World of Change," Brigham Young University, June 7, 1967.

"Genealogy: A Priesthood Responsibility," genealogical seminar, Brigham Young University, June 22, 1967.

Graduation address, LDS Institute of Religion, Utah State University, May 18, 1975.

"A Leader Has Faith," article prepared for *Instructor,* 1966.

"Leadership: Our Challenge Today," Explorer leadership seminar, Brigham Young University, August 20, 1967.

"The Principles of the Gospel Are Eternal," general conference address, October 4, 1966.

Address to missionaries, Valparaiso, Chile, November 2, 1967.

Genealogy

"Genealogy: A Priesthood Responsibility," genealogical seminar, Brigham Young University, June 22, 1967.

The Holy Ghost

"The Continuing Power of the Holy Ghost," general conference address, April 8, 1971.

Honesty

"Choose the Right," address to Latter-day Saints Student Association, University of Utah, November 17, 1972.

Joseph Smith

"Modern Revelation," general conference address, April 6, 1965.

Justice and Mercy

"The Eternal Gospel Principles of Justice, Mercy, and Humility," general conference address, April 4, 1970.

Leadership

Commencement address, Brigham Young University, August 21, 1969.

"Excellence," commencement address, Benemerito de las Americas, August 23, 1968.

Graduation address, LDS Institute of Religion, Utah State University, May 18, 1975.

"Leadership: Our Challenge Today," area conference, Buenos Aires, Argentina, March 9, 1975.

"Opportunities for Leadership Ingenuity," address to business students, Brigham Young University, April 12, 1962.

Love

"The Abundant Life through Service," address to missionaries, 1960.

"Genealogy: A Priesthood Responsibility," genealogical seminar, Brigham Young University, June 22, 1967.

"Love, Service, and Spiritual Achievement," Brigham Young University, December 14, 1965.

Loyalty

"Loyalty," general conference address, April 4, 1969.

Missionaries and Missionary Work

Address to missionaries, Cambridge, Massachusetts, May 12, 1962.

Address to missionaries, Valparaiso, Chile, November 2, 1967.

"Amazing Growth," general conference address, October 1, 1961.

"Giving One's All," general conference address, April 5, 1964.

"Have a Dream," *New Era*, January 1978, p. 4.

"How to Do Missionary Work," Lessons A and B, *Melchizedek Priesthood Study Manual*, 1970-71.

"Leadership: Our Challenge Today," Explorer leadership seminar, Brigham Young University, August 20, 1967.

"Make Your Dreams Come True," address to Salt Lake area seminary students, March 22, 1974.

"New but Old," general conference address, October 5, 1962.

Missionary Efforts by Members

Address to missionaries, Cambridge, Massachusetts, May 21, 1962.

"Amazing Growth," general conference address, October 1, 1961.

"Be a Missionary," general conference address, April 7, 1962.

"Effective Missionary Work: Every Member a Missionary," mission presidents seminar, June 23, 1982.

"Every Member a Missionary," general conference address, October 4, 1963.

"How to Do Missionary Work," Lessons A and B, *Melchizedek Priesthood Study Manual*, 1970-71.

"Lengthening Your Stride as a Missionary," general conference address, April 1977.

"New but Old," general conference address, October 5, 1962.

"Share the Gospel," general conference address, April 8, 1961.

Motherhood

"Motherhood," Chevy Chase Ward, Washington (D.C.) Stake, May 10, 1953.

Obedience

"Excellence," Brigham Young University, July 11, 1972.

"Thy Will Be Done, O Lord, and Not Ours," general conference address, October 7, 1972.

Parenthood

Talk to parents at area conference, Buenos Aires, Argentina, March 8, 1975.

Patience

"Patience: An Essential Virtue," general conference address, April 5, 1968.

Perfecting the Saints

"Perfecting the Saints," general conference address, October 1, 1976.

Prayer

"Genealogy: A Priesthood Responsibility," genealogical seminar, Brigham Young University, June 22, 1967.

"The Importance of Prayer," general conference address, April 8, 1972.

Reactivation

"Giving One's All," general conference address, April 5, 1964.

"Seek Not for Riches but for Wisdom," general conference address, April 3, 1976.

"Talents: A Blessing and Responsibility," general conference address, October 6, 1968.

Resurrection

"Easter and the Latter-day Saints," *Deseret News*, April 9, 1950.

"The Message of Easter," general conference address, April 5, 1975.

Reverence

"How to Improve Reverence and Worship in Church," General Authorities report meeting, March 6, 1969.

Sacrifice

"Giving One's All," general conference address, April 5, 1964.

Graduation address, LDS Institute of Religion, Utah State University, May 18, 1975.

"Our First and Second Estates," general conference address, October 3, 1965.

Sacrament meeting talk, East Millcreek Eighth Ward, Mount Olympus Stake, July 26, 1970.

"Sacrifice Brings Forth the Blessings of Heaven," general conference address, April 3, 1967.

Scripture Study

Priesthood board meeting, May 19, 1976.

Talents

"Building the Kingdom," address at Sao Paulo and Buenos Aires area conferences, March 1 and 8, 1975.

Graduation address, LDS Institute of Religion, Utah State University, May 18, 1975.

"Make Your Dreams Come True," address to Salt Lake area seminary students, March 22, 1974.

"Talents: A Blessing and Responsibility," general conference address, October 6, 1968.

Temples

Dedication services address, Washington Temple, November 20, 1974.

Testimony

"Love, Service, and Spiritual Achievement," Brigham Young University, December 14, 1965.

"Testimony," general conference address, April 6, 1974.

Thanksgiving

"Thanksgiving," Salt Lake Rotary Club, November 20, 1962.

Tithing

Friend to Friend: General Authorities Speak to Children (Deseret Book, 1977), pp. 16-18.

"The Law of Abundance," general conference address, April 3, 1971.

Wealth

"Be Humble and Strong," general conference address, October 4, 1965.

"The Law of Abundance," general conference address, April 3, 1971.

Work

Friend to Friend: General Authorities Speak to Children (Deseret Book, 1977), pp. 16-18.

"The Gospel of Work," general conference address, October 5, 1969.

Sacrament meeting talk, East Millcreek Eighth Ward, Mount Olympus Stake, July 26, 1970.

Index